DREAM BIG
& Imagine the What If

Kylie Captain

First published by Ultimate World Publishing 2021
Copyright © 2021 Kylie Captain

ISBN

Paperback: 978-1-922597-75-5
Ebook: 978-1-922597-76-2

Kylie Captain has asserted her rights under the Copyright, Designs and Patents Act 1988 to be identified as the author of this work. The information in this book is based on the author's experiences and opinions. The publisher specifically disclaims responsibility for any adverse consequences which may result from use of the information contained herein. Permission to use information has been sought by the author. Any breaches will be rectified in further editions of the book.

All rights reserved. No part of this publication may be reproduced, stored in or introduced into a retrieval system, or transmitted in any form, or by any means (electronic, mechanical, photocopying, recording or otherwise) without the prior written permission of the author. Any person who does any unauthorised act in relation to this publication may be liable to criminal prosecution and civil claims for damages. Enquiries should be made through the publisher.

Cover design: Michael Fardon
Layout and typesetting: Ultimate World Publishing
Editor: Alex Floyd-Douglass

Ultimate World Publishing
Diamond Creek,
Victoria Australia 3089
www.writeabook.com.au

For Tyrell and Allira.

My inspiration for everything I do. By far, my greatest achievement has and will always be you.

To my husband, none of this would be possible without you.

To my angels who continue to guide and comfort me in spirit, thank you for your ongoing love and protection.

I hope I've made you proud.

ACKNOWLEDGEMENT

I acknowledge and pay respect to the Traditional Custodians and Elders right across this beautiful Country. I thank them for allowing me to live, work and visit their spiritual lands. I acknowledge my ancestors and old people for their continuous guidance and protection as I go about my work educating and inspiring our young people to believe in themselves and chase their dreams.

DISCLAIMER

Aboriginal and Torres Strait Islander readers are advised that this book contains the names and photos of people who are deceased.

This book contains the memories and opinions of the author. The author's memories and feelings are those of her own and the author acknowledges that readers may have different opinions and beliefs.

The strategies used and suggested by the author do not intend to replace professional advice.

Testimonies written in this book are the opinions of the individual.

The author uses Aboriginal English throughout the book and some words are misspelt intentionally. Please refer to the glossary where needed.

The author uses the terms Aboriginal People and Aboriginal Peoples as there is no single Aboriginal or Torres Strait Islander identity.

The author acknowledges this diversity and for the purpose of this book which is told in her own voice, using her own thoughts and opinions, she uses the terms Aboriginal or Aboriginal peoples in line with her own dialogue and where it best suits the tone and intent of the story.

TESTIMONIALS

"Being from the Gumilaroi community of Walgett, I share a common cultural and family heritage with Kylie Captain and reading her story fills me with profound pride and admiration.

I know Kylie's family and the pain of loss.

Kylie's book, *Dream Big and Imagine the What If* should be compulsory reading for all who are willing to dream and those who refuse to allow adversity to define them.

Kylie's story stands as testament to overcoming adversity and the strength of dreams and of believing.

Kylie's book is filled with messages of kin and Country; it celebrates the intrinsic power of dreams and gratitude and it is a moving chronicle of resilience.

Kylie is the woman she has become because she refused to surrender to adversity. I am so proud of her brave resilience and her survival and her book is there to inspire, motivate and serve as a signpost for the possibility of hope and the transformative magic of dreams.

Read the book and be empowered."

Professor Bob Morgan
Respected Aboriginal Educator,
Researcher and Social Justice Advocate

"Kylie's story should be read by every educator, every student, indeed every Australian. It's a story of determination, grit and commitment, of an awakening to the emancipatory power of education to mobilise new ideas, opportunities and possibilities.

It is also a story of the strength, resilience, respect and reciprocity embedded in Aboriginal communities, of a First Nations people who refuse assimilation as the best option and push forward against enormous pressure to assert their cultural, political and sovereign rights.

Kylie's story is the embodiment of this strength and gives us all hope that if we listen to and learn from First Nations peoples and communities, if we embrace the generosity and wisdom of educators like Kylie, we as Australians and as a nation will learn from our past and mature into the nation we should be, a sustainable, authentic and empathetic diverse community of leaders and innovators."

Associate Professor Cathie Burgess
University of Sydney, President Aboriginal Studies Association

Testimonials

"Kylie's rawness, honesty and truth is both inspiring and motivating.

As an Aboriginal woman, her words leapt out of the page and into my heart pulling on the strings of similarities. Her resilience and positivity as a strong and proud black woman have changed the trajectory of her path.

Each chapter of her journey is steeped in connection with people and country. Overlaid with eternal gratefulness she has shaped the darkest moments into spaces of challenge and growth. Never a woman to walk away from a challenge and someone who takes the time to share and encourage others. I'm forever thankful to call her a sista, colleague and friend.

She is both powerfully wonderful and solidly black. It's without a doubt a must read."

Tammy Anderson
Aboriginal Educational Leader

"To Dream Big and Imagine the What If is not only the title of this book but the mantra in which Kylie has chosen to live her life. Kylie's journey is a story of determination, resilience, strength and hope and one I encourage everyone to read.

Kylie is a strong, proud, Aboriginal woman who prioritises her time on improving outcomes for her mob. Kylie stands on the shoulders of her Elders and through her yarns shares the importance of "every child deserves a champion: an adult who will never give up on them, who understands the power of connection and insists they become the best they can possibly be" (Rita Pierson).

Throughout this story Kylie shares the many challenges she has faced throughout her life and the lessons learnt to rise above. A story that has you feeling every emotion, but leaves you inspired and motivated to dream big and live the best life you can!"

Natalie Pierson
Aboriginal Educational Leader

Testimonials

"'Time waits for no one. Break the cycle and dream big for a better and brighter future for you and your mob' (Kylie Captain).

Tragedy, sacrifice and injustice can crush the soul. How much can one person truly survive before they are swept away into the numbing depth of despair? Author, educator and proud Gamilaroi woman, Kylie Captain, lays bare the visceral and raw personal story of loss and circumstance.

When all is lost but hope. The strength of hope to not dismiss or erase what has happened in life but to believe it can be better. To explore the positivity of 'What if'. Reading this book is not just good for your soul, it is the 'old-fashioned blackfulla curry chicken soup' you need in this uncertain world we live in.

Kylie Captain has shown not only how to be a champion of her culture and living life big, but how to harness all that is good in life and to spread the cosmic karma of kindness, education, wisdom and love to others.

I feel that Kylie was meant to be in my life to lift me and to encourage me to be better and to be a strong ally for our Aboriginal brothers and sisters. A heartbreaking but incredible read from a resilient and inspiring author."

Mike Newcombe
Educational Leader

"Kylie was meant to write this story. Through her raw, genuine and compelling narrative, Kylie provides a road map of life lessons and strategies to help us as individuals, as a community and as a nation."

Maria Serafim
Educational Leader

CONTENTS

Acknowledgement	v
Disclaimer	vii
Testimonials	ix
Introduction	1
Chapter One: We All Have a Story	5
Chapter Two: Riding the Waves of Grief	41
Chapter Three: Black and Proud	55
Chapter Four: Breaking the Cycle	87
Chapter Five: From Fear to Resilience	101
Chapter Six: Imagine the 'What If'	107
Chapter Seven: The Change Starts Now	139
Chapter Eight: The Teacher in All of Us	147
Chapter Nine: Everyone Deserves a Champion	159
Chapter Ten: Deadly Secrets to Success	169
Chapter Eleven: Whether You Think You Can, or You Can't, You're Right	183
Chapter Twelve: What I Know For Sure	193
About the Author	211
About the Artist (book cover)	213
Acknowledgements	217
Glossary	221
Kylie's Deadly Chicken Soup	223
Further Testimonials	225

INTRODUCTION

The tearing of a picture; a moment knowing that I would never be that person again. The image, still clear in my mind and makes me sick to the stomach with guilt and shame for allowing myself to fall so low. Fear of knowing how close I was to becoming stuck in a vicious cycle and heading down a path of self-destruction …

The picture is of me as a 15 year old sitting on my grandmother's lounge. I had a bong in my right hand and a bowl of yarndi on my lap. I sat slumped on the couch, stoned out of my head and staring into space. I looked terribly thin and lost with no hope or direction in life. The sad part is that my Nan was just a few metres away, sitting in the dining room playing cards with the old girls from our community. She couldn't see me but the fact that I was in her house in that state brings me to tears.

The guilt and shame, still so present in my heart.

I found this picture years later and immediately tore it up in disgust and in fear that my children may one day find it. I didn't want them to see me like that. I was embarrassed about my past and too ashamed to ever let anyone know about it.

We all have a story and some of us have many stories. My story is one of resilience and hope. Hope to live a life of freedom and choice, despite the many challenges that have been thrown my way.

Today, I am a proud Aboriginal woman, a passionate educational leader, a homeowner, a confident public speaker, an author and a changemaker. I am a world traveller and, importantly, a teacher. I have had a near-death experience and have what they call a life-threatening heart condition which requires me to have an Internal Cardiac Defibrillator. This is something I'll live with for the rest of my life. I am a survivor of many of life's assignments, and I'm proud to say that I've smashed out each and every one of them.

In my other story, things were very different for me. I was someone with no aspirations or hope for the future. At times, I was very sick in hospital, hated life and often thought, *"Why me?"*

As a teen, I struggled with addiction, would shoplift for basic necessities, often scared, sad and ashamed. I've experienced unimaginable grief and loss due to the passing of several significant people in my life.

I'm proud to say that I have survived.

Introduction

I'm here to share my story in the hope to inspire and motivate anyone who wants to hit the reset button and start dreaming big to create a life and future on their terms. I share my story for our youth and those who have a past they are not proud of or a past that has been full of challenges. I share because I want everyone to know that our past does not have to dictate our future.

It doesn't matter how many times we chose the wrong path, there is always a chance to redirect and explore the possibilities that await on the path less travelled.

Throughout this book, I will share some of those 'what if' moments that have shaped me into the strong, proud, resilient woman I am today. I have always been a dreamer and can vividly recall many times when I had such moments.

For a lot of us, when we think of the words 'what if', our minds often go to those fearful or negative thoughts, as fear has a way of numbing us and stopping us in our tracks. We might often think, *"What if things don't turn out well?"* or *"What if something bad happens?"*

I'm here to flip those 'what if's' on their head and encourage you to imagine the 'what if' in a positive light. Like, *"What if I get that deadly job?"* or *"What if I can still have a good life despite all these challenges?"* or *"What if I can travel the world and complete that university degree despite not feeling like I'm good enough?"*

Those 'what ifs' were my story. I have now found my courage and finally feel brave enough to share parts of it with you. I will share some of the strategies I've used to help me live an abundant life full of good health and happiness: two things we all strive for and are absolutely entitled to.

In this book, I will weave through my story as we touch on topics such as Aboriginality, breaking the cycle, education, grief and the law of attraction. I share my insight and the strategies and lessons I've learnt to inspire, motivate and support anyone who wants to make a positive change in life. I also want to use this opportunity to educate and raise awareness about Australia's true history and to inspire teachers to never stop believing in our kids.

This book encourages you to reflect on where you are, where you want to be, and most importantly, the things you are prepared to do to achieve your dreams and goals.

If I can give hope to and inspire just one person, my heart will be full. My dream is to leave a legacy that my story has positively impacted the lives of others. I want to be remembered as someone who was brave and resilient and someone who never gave up.

This is my story of dreaming big and imagining the 'what if'.

Chapter One

WE ALL HAVE A STORY

I was an only child, and sadly my birth mother, Millie, passed away when I was three years old. I was raised by my aunty, who stepped in and became my mother. She was mostly a single mum of four girls – including me.

I grew up in housing commission flats in Waterloo, an inner-city community of Sydney where many of us struggled. I missed a lot of school due to suffering from chronic psoriasis, a debilitating autoimmune disease that at times left me covered in thick silvery scales and in hospital for weeks on end. I suffered from the age of 10 right through to my adult years.

By 14, I was heavily addicted to yarndi and I would smoke from the minute I opened my eyes till the moment I eventually fell asleep. All the drug dealers around Waterloo and Redfern knew me. I became so addicted that I was no longer affected by the drug, no matter how much I smoked. This led me to dabble with heroin, a drug which unfortunately had already taken the lives of many in my community.

Thankfully, this isn't my story anymore and hasn't been for a long time.

There were a few miracle moments that changed my life. One in particular was a teacher who supported me in completing my Higher School Certificate (HSC).

Being the first in my family to complete the HSC was a huge achievement. At such a critical crossroads in my life, it was a teacher who made a difference for me.

I am who I am today because someone believed in me.

Someone told me that I was good enough and smart enough to do anything I set my mind to. It is because of this teacher that I decided to pursue a career in education. I thought it was only right that I pay it forward as without that kindness, I wouldn't be where I am today.

Throughout my younger years, I was heading down a very negative path. I slipped into a bad habit of shoplifting. I would steal things like deodorant and perfumes, then went on to clothes and shoes for my niece and nephews and ended up stealing anything I could get my hands on.

I got caught in Grace Bros when I was about 14. I had my two year old nephew in the pram at the time. The police phoned my Nan to let her know that I had been caught and there were lots of F-words coming through on the other end of that phone. I went home feeling proud of the fact that they let me off with a warning – and because they didn't find the kids' socks that I had stashed in my armpits.

I often reflect on that moment and wonder how things may have turned out if I had been charged, as so many Aboriginal kids are charged for minor things that change the entire trajectory of their life.

My past is not something that I'm proud of. I would do anything to change that part of my story, but it's all the parts of my story that make me who I am. I share purely to make a difference for others. To remind teachers and adults to never give up on a child.

Growing up, I was always really nice and polite. However, I was very shy in my younger years and never liked to talk much. I always felt shame, like many of us black kids – with strangers, anyway. At home, I was wild and crazy.

My sadness and hard times started early in life. When I was 10, my psoriasis flared up. I was covered from head to toe and would be hospitalised for weeks at a time. My family had never seen psoriasis before and didn't know how to treat it. I remember Mum trialling all of her home remedies, but it quickly got out of control.

Eventually, I had an appointment at the Children's Hospital and was diagnosed which had an extremely negative impact on my life. The stares I would get from people were embarrassing and heartbreaking.

My self-esteem was low and some of those sick kids in hospital did a good job of letting me know how different I was. They would see me covered in bandages and call me names like *"Mummy!"* or *"Freak!"*

I hated my time there. Every day was the same: oil baths, ultraviolet light therapy, disgustingly scented creams and wet dressings. Each day, I would wake to my bed full of scales and bloodstained sheets from the intense scratching in my sleep. I did an excellent job of covering it up, though.

I lived in long pants and long sleeves to hide my disgusting skin. I remember travelling to Walgett in the summer when I was about 13. I was in a jumper and tracksuit pants, suffering from heat stroke as I couldn't handle the heat. People would look at me as though I was mad for wearing winter clothes in the peak of summer.

I smoked yarndi and would binge drink right throughout my teens and until I fell pregnant with my son at 18. He was a blessing in disguise and came into my life just when I needed him most. I was heading down a path of self-destruction. I had no hope or aspirations for anything positive in the future.

I believe my son actually saved my life.

My First Heartbreak

My beautiful mother, Millie May Captain, was just 28 when she passed away peacefully in her sleep. This was my first heartbreak and one that still sits heavy in my heart. Feelings

I've buried deep within have started to resurface as I write. Mum was a patient of the famous Dr Victor Chang and I'm devastated that there wasn't something they could do to save her.

When Mum was diagnosed with her heart condition, my family moved from Walgett to Sydney to be closer to the specialists. She was under the most incredible team of health care professionals and she had a pacemaker, but for some reason, she didn't get the chance to live beyond her short 28 years.

She was kind and loving and everyone who knew her speaks so highly of her. I only have a few memories of my mother; flashbacks that often pop into my mind when I least expect them.

The first is where I was playing with some other kids in Nan's front yard. My mum was standing on the other side of the fence, reaching over to lock the gate. She's smiling, telling me that she was going to the shop and asking me what flavour ice block I wanted. I looked up at her and said I wanted a lemonade ice block. The sun was shining, and she looked like an angel staring down at me. I can still see her beautiful smiling face and lovely long, dark hair. Unfortunately, I can't quite remember the sound of her voice, and for years, I've wondered what she sounded like.

I would give anything to hear her voice again.

The second vision I have is of her lying in bed after she passed. I remember my grandfather telling me to go upstairs to ask

Mum if she wanted a cup of tea. I remember taking the big steps up the very steep stairs in my Nan's terrace house, then climbing up onto the bed trying to wake her. She wouldn't wake up.

She was resting so peacefully and looked like she was in prayer.

The third memory is of someone holding me in the corner of Nan's lounge room where there was a group of people gathered. I recall two people carrying a stretcher down the steep stairs and out the front door. I can still feel the sadness in the room.

These are the only memories I have of my mother. I am told she was an amazing woman who touched the hearts of many.

The stories and few photos of Mum are things I have always treasured. I am lucky to have the most beautiful portrait of us which was taken not long before she passed. Her beautiful nature shines through, as does her love for me. I know how much she loved and adored me. People say I always looked immaculate and never had a hair out of place.

I am often told how much I look like her.

When I go to Walgett, our family and her old friends are often shocked as they refer to me as the *"spitting image"* of her. This makes me smile and fills my heart with pride as it's where I've always felt her. From a very young age, I developed a spiritual connection to my mother.

Even now, I'm always talking to her and seeking guidance when needed.

Throughout my early years of primary school, I carried the grief of losing my mum. Teachers would often see me sitting in the corner, crying on significant days like Mother's Day or her birthday. I remember saying that I felt sad because it was a special day, but my mum had passed away.

One thing I am forever grateful for is the fact that I never grew up without the love of a mother.

Mum had one sister and when she passed away, Mum Denise stepped in and became my mother. Her three daughters became my sisters, and she raised me as her own. Mum Denise loved me with all her heart and she was always so proud of everything that I had achieved in life.

Sadly, she passed away in 2011. I will treasure her memory and the love we shared for all of my days.

The Love of a Grandmother Is Like No Other

I was blessed to have had my beautiful Nan, Delphine, for the first 16 years of my life. She was my best friend. We shared a connection that is like nothing I have ever experienced.

A love only a grandmother can give.

When Nan passed away, I felt like my heart had been broken into a million pieces. All the questions that I still had for her and all the milestones I wanted her to be around for were no more. I sat at her hospital bed for the next 11 days after her stroke. I wouldn't leave her room. My family would bring me what I needed; however, I refused to leave. Nan held on for 11 days after she was taken off life support.

I believe she didn't want to pass while I was there.

On day 11, I told her I was going home to get a feed and to grab a few things. I said I'd be back in an hour. I told her how much I loved her, and I kissed her and left.

When I returned, I was told that she was gone.

I can still hear her laugh and all the songs she sang to me as a child. She always had a Bible beside her bed and knew all these beautiful Christian songs. We'd lie in bed together, singing and laughing. She had the most incredible sense of humour, which still makes me laugh when I think of her. She was Patsy Cline's biggest fan and would have her records blaring all day while she sat in front of the heater with her cup of tea. Nan loved wearing beautiful, colourful dresses and matching necklaces. She was a social butterfly and loved nothing more than sitting on her front porch talking to anyone who walked past.

I was usually beside her, sitting on the step. She would tell all these strangers that I was her granddaughter and talk about how proud she was. She would have her *Meals on Wheels* delivered and the desserts and juices were always for me. No one else was allowed to touch them. She always made me feel so special and loved.

I did my part to help care for her as she was in a wheelchair after suffering a stroke. She was also set on fire while she played two-up one ANZAC Day. She had horrific scars on her body that broke my heart every day. I don't know too much about this story, other than the fact that it was traumatic and left my Nan and those around her with a deep sense of sadness.

My beautiful Nan was a survivor. I loved her with all my heart.

Myself and many others were often seen wheeling her to and from The Block so she could play her beloved cards. She was a pretty deadly card player and I hear she was an incredible pool player in her younger years.

Nan was lucky enough to return to Worrabinda a few years before she passed. Her friend Beth organised to get her there. This trip was something Nan wanted to do for a long time. She tried her best to arrange a plane ticket for me too; however, there simply wasn't enough money. I loved seeing the photos and hearing the yarns about her trip.

Nan was so happy – her spirit felt restored.

After Nan passed, my heart was broken.

My drug-taking and irresponsible behaviour continued, and I felt like my life was spiralling out of control.

A Big and Special Heart

At 17, I had a near-death experience. My cardiologist said that I was lucky to survive. How I didn't drop dead, he doesn't know. The erratic and dangerous heart rhythms he witnessed was beyond scary and why I'm still alive is a question only God knows.

My near-death experience was self-inflicted due to excessive alcohol use, which caused days of vomiting from alcohol poisoning. These events led to the diagnosis of my life-threatening heart condition called Long QT syndrome, an electrical condition of the heart that affects its rhythm and can cause fast, chaotic heartbeats and sudden death.

In my teens, many of us kids would drink for entertainment. A local pub in my area sold us underage kids cheap, no-name alcohol without labels. After a few glasses, we'd often be vomiting or passed out.

When I was diagnosed with my heart condition, I remember feeling so sick and being terribly thin. I recall being weighed at the hospital and weighed only 47kg. For my height, I was extremely thin. I was in the coronary care ward full of elderly people. When Mum would visit, I could see the fear in her eyes. She was terrified that history would repeat itself and I, too, would be taken just like my birth mother. She would bring my niece and nephews and little treats to try and cheer me up.

I remember feeling so miserable and, at times, would struggle just to keep my eyes open.

When I was 18, I was legally allowed into pubs and clubs, and my careless life continued. All I looked forward to week after week was getting drunk and partying. My tolerance to alcohol became extremely high. I could drink all night, starting in the afternoon and going through till lunchtime the next day. I sometimes put myself in dangerous situations, and my friends, who I used to party with, knew how clumsy I was. I was always falling over. I'm lucky I didn't seriously hurt myself. I ended up with all sorts of minor injuries, such as a grazed face and I even lost half a tooth. My cousin, Bronwyn, and I still laugh about that story; however, I'm lucky I didn't end up with far more serious injuries when I think about it.

It was my excessive drinking that triggered my heart condition that was always there. I'm glad I was diagnosed because many people with my condition often die suddenly with no previous symptoms or a diagnosis.

After my diagnosis, I was prescribed medication and monitored every six months by my cardiologist who coincidentally was an intern treating my mum, alongside Dr Victor Chang. He recognised the name and mentioned how much I looked like my mum. He is one of Sydney's leading cardiologists and he has treated me for the past 23 years. I am forever grateful for my deadly doctor, who has looked after me all of these years.

When I was 23, he became very concerned about my heart and decided it was best to have an Implanted Cardiac Defibrillator (ICD). The ICD is an electrical box that sits inside my chest. Being a young mum with two children by this stage, I didn't hesitate to undergo the procedure. The ICD sits in the left side of my chest and I have wires screwed into my heart which would hopefully zap me back if I were to die suddenly. This is an operation I've had three times in the last 16 years. I like to think of myself as a bionic woman; a little energiser bunny who can just go go go!

I was terrified of my ICD in the early years as I read stories of them going off by accident and zapping you. I didn't engage in exercise and tried my best to keep my heart rate low as people describe the zap like getting kicked in the chest by a horse (don't ask me how they know what that feels like) and it most certainly causes you to pass out. Despite the fear around my defibrillator, I'm grateful for it as I'm confident that if my mother had one, she may still be alive today.

The Early Years

When I think of home, I think of those tall units in Waterloo where I lived for the first 19 years of my life. I grew up in the Drysdale Housing Commission flats, on the corner of Pitt and Wellington. We didn't have much; however, I wouldn't change it for a thing.

All of my experiences have shaped me into the woman I am today.

I lived with Mum Denise and my three sisters, Tanya, Narelle and Kathy. My niece Kira and nephews, Trent, Jon, Nathan and Duane, then came along, and our home was a busy place, full of laughter and good times. I enjoyed nothing more than being an aunty, a job and title I loved and took seriously. I cared for and loved my niece and nephews as though they were my own. They really did bring so much joy to my life.

Mum was a kind woman who always had an open-door policy. Any of my sisters' friends or family from the country were always welcome at our house.

Our home was always filled with a big mob of extended family from Walgett or friends from the community.

I barely remember our front door being locked and people were always coming and going. We weren't fussed about sleeping in bedrooms, and the couch always had someone on it. There was usually a soup on the stove and mattresses on the lounge room floor. Hot chips and bread were a staple for many of us in Waterloo. $2 could feed a big mob of us. I bet that takeaway shop made a killing from our community.

I am forever grateful that Mum raised me as her own after my birth mother passed away. She allowed me to experience growing up black and provided me with all the love and nurturing I needed.

My father, Mick, is a white man, and when I think about it, things could have easily turned out differently for me if my dad had taken me after Mum passed away.

My Aboriginality is where I draw my strength and resilience. It's hard to describe the feelings of pride, culture, spirituality and connection I get from being Aboriginal. It is who I am, and I can't imagine what life would be like without that connection.

Whilst I've never lived with my dad, he'd visit when he could and take me to visit my family, who I love and appreciate. My dad has always been so proud of me, and I'm grateful to have him in my life.

Kinship is one of the most beautiful things that I love about my culture, as it is so important in our communities. We look after each other and step in and take on that parental responsibility where needed. In my case, I was never denied the love of a mother. I loved growing up in a wild and crazy household with my older sisters and the rest of my mob.

The love Mum showed me is hard to describe. She and I had the most beautiful connection. She wasn't allowed to go to the pub until I was asleep. She would have to lie on the mattress with me until I dozed off. If I felt her trying to sneak off I would run to the door and create a barricade, so she couldn't get past. I would hold on to the rail next to the door and stretch out my legs on to the door to prevent her from opening it. She would try to tickle me to get me to move; however, it never worked. She was never allowed to leave until I was asleep. She was always laughing at the silly things I would do.

I was so full of energy, always dancing and running up and down our balcony. I was the baby of the family and I was so proud of it. My older sisters would often describe me as spoilt as I could do no wrong in Mum's eyes. She was the most beautiful, kind and caring woman I've ever met and I'm forever grateful to have had her in my life.

Mum loved country music and, like Nan, was a deadly pool player. She was often winning pool comps at the local pubs.

She was always so proud of her achievements. Like many black families, we loved listening to country music. Some of my favourite memories were when we travelled to Tamworth to attend the Country Music Festival.

I met my best friend, Johanna, through country music as she and her family were performers. Since about the age of 10, we've been the best of friends. I refer to her as my white sister. We have the most beautiful connection, and I'm forever grateful to have her in my life. I'd often stay with her family in Tamworth during the festival. I would wait while she busked and we would then use the money to buy ice cream and play games at the local arcade. Johanna has the most incredible voice, and I've always loved listening to her sing. She has been a source of strength and support through everything I've experienced. I will always be her number one fan.

Although we struggled financially, Mum always found a way to make ends meet. We were your typical black family living with the challenges many other Aboriginal families in our community faced. As a child, I would sometimes think about what I wanted to do or achieve when I grew up, and I remember thinking that I couldn't wait to apply for my own housing commission place. I hoped that I would be given a house with a yard as I was sick of living in a unit. However, not once can I recall thinking about the possibility of buying a home as I didn't know anyone in our community who owned their own home.

I thought that housing options for our people were limited and property ownership was only for rich, white people.

As a child, I attended Redfern Public School, which had a big mob of us black kids from the Redfern and Waterloo community. I enjoyed school in my younger years; however, I was that kid who always seemed to struggle. I was absent a lot of the time due to travelling to and from the country, being in hospital – or simply not wanting to go to school.

I was a child who lacked confidence and didn't ever think I was good enough or smart enough. I wasn't sporty and didn't feel pretty. We didn't have much, but I had the basics to get by, which is all I needed.

I loved playing and hanging out with my friends. We would do handstands and have so much fun playing games like elastics and tips. However, there was always this daunting dread as well. Dread about not wanting to be there because I didn't feel smart. I often felt like I was the dumbest kid in the class.

Mum would walk me halfway to school, across all the roads until we got to the park. She would then watch me as I walked the rest of the way. I would stop every few steps to turn back and wave. She would stand there smiling and waving up. She reckons I was so slow and that it would have been faster if she would have walked me all the way – haha.

We had a Koori room at school where us kids could go and grab a sandwich or a piece of fruit if we needed it. I'd only go sometimes, as most of the time I was too shame. The only reason I wanted to go was so I could grab an apple to feed the police horse that was at our zebra crossing after school.

One time, the horse bit my fingers. He had a tight hold and wouldn't let go. The officer had to get off the horse and give him a whack with his baton. I went home crying with my sore fingers. Mum couldn't help but laugh as it was only a minor injury. She said, *"That's what you get for wanting to feed that horse; you should have eaten it yourself."*

I remember being enrolled at Walgett Public School in Year Five during an extended visit after attending a funeral. My basic literacy and numeracy skills were appalling. I remember one of my peers saying, *"Geez, I thought you city kids were smart,"* and they got a real confidence boost from seeing how far behind I was.

I honestly felt like there was something wrong with me. At Redfern Public School, I remember myself and a few others being transported to the hospital to attend a special reading program. There were only about three of us in the car, and whilst it was fun and exciting to be doing this 'special' program, I remember the terrible impact it had on my self-esteem.

As time went on, I didn't want to be at school. I always felt like there was so much to catch up on, especially towards my later primary years when I was diagnosed with psoriasis. I would sit up the back of the class and not want to participate in the learning. At times, the teacher would just give me a dot-to-dot or colouring-in task to do, while the rest of the class moved on with the learning. That embedded my belief about not being smart and having trouble learning.

I often stayed home on pension day to go to the bank to withdraw Nan's money and pay her bills. Playing cards for money was popular within the Redfern and Waterloo community. On pension day, Nan was either down The Block or there would be a big mob at her house where everyone from the community would gather. The room was always filled with so much humour.

Blackfullas truly are the funniest.

The yarns, the stories, were all full of animation and great detail. I loved sitting around watching and listening. Nan and Mum would say children should be seen and not heard, so I tried my best to be quiet; however, most of the time, I was full of energy, making people laugh and going on silly.

Growing up with my Aboriginal family provided me with a deep understanding of life and the struggles some of our people face.

My culture runs deep within my soul. My connection to my ancestors and family members who have passed is strong, and I often seek their spiritual guidance, love and support to help navigate my way through life.

I grew up in a community that was strong and resilient. Everyone looked out for each other. We were like one big family. I have so many memories of us kids playing in the park or knock and run in the high-rise flats. I love reminiscing with my brothers and sistas from my community about all the yarns and happy memories from those days.

I also came from a community that struggled, and it was easy to become a product of your environment. When I started smoking yarndi, it made me sick to the point of sitting in the gutter vomiting those first few times. However, I persevered and before long, I started to understand why so many loved it. It was numbing and calming and helped take away any fear and anxiety I had inside.

It saddens me, and I'm ashamed to say that I was once a drug addict and a thief with no dreams or aspirations for the future. I would cry if I didn't have drugs and would go anywhere to find what I needed. Drugs came first, even before food. I couldn't even eat until I was high because I felt sick. I would smoke every day.

I often look around and think of my life now which is one of freedom and choice and feel like that past life was all a dream.

My past has shaped me into the grateful person I am today. When I turn on the tap in the morning, and there is hot water running, I am grateful.

There were times when we couldn't afford our bills and the gas and electricity would be turned off. Mum always did her best to sort it quickly; however, those times without it makes me appreciate those little things in life we often take for granted.

When I go to sleep at night feeling safe and warm, I'm grateful.

When I have a cooked meal and see my kids happy and healthy, I'm grateful.

I see myself as having an unsettled spirit, always wanting to do more and be more. I am someone who has strived to be the best possible version of myself, to live life on my terms, not defined by the tragedies or circumstances that have been thrown my way.

I think back and see visions of my sister, Narelle, who was always so bubbly. She had such a beautiful personality, and her interpersonal skills were amazing. She knew how to talk to anyone. Narelle had a few deadly jobs working at Centrelink and Sydney Water, and she took me and her son Trent on our first holiday to the Gold Coast. I remember hearing how Narelle had achieved her Year 10 Certificate and I looked up to her as a role model. She was fun and someone who loved life.

Sadly, when I think about the grief I've experienced and the people close to me who I've lost, Narelle is part of that story. My heart still aches for my sister, who passed away when she was just 30 years old. Narelle's infectious smile and love of life is part of my story. I learnt so much from my sister and I'm forever grateful for having her in my life.

Not a day goes by that I don't think of her and see her beautiful smile.

Narelle's passing resulted in me becoming a carer for her son. For a period of time, at just 21, I was the guardian of my 12 year old nephew whilst raising my two year old son. My nephew means the world to me, and I'm honoured to have been here all these years as a support for him in my sisters' absence.

Not long before Narelle passed, I lost one of my best friends to suicide. I think of her often and wonder what she'd be doing now. She was the happiest of us all which makes me care deeply for others as you never know what people are hiding inside.

There is a lot of intergenerational trauma that's been passed down and, sadly, it's still happening today.

Mum never had nice things to say about white people because of her experience of growing up in a town that was full of racism where many blackfullas weren't allowed in the pools, movies, clubs and for some, even school. Mum only went to school until she was 11, and then she was out working on cattle stations for white families. She remembers being told she wasn't allowed to attend school and had to go off to work.

The segregation and discrimination of my people was horrific, and it wasn't until Mum was 15 years old that she finally became a citizen of this country. Before the 1967 referendum, she was not considered a human being like every other blackfulla. Mum grew up on Namoi Reserve in Walgett and had lots of amazing memories playing by the river and living in their little tin shack. She described her time growing up as a happy one, living with her community and extended family, who treated each other like brothers and sisters.

I'm forever grateful to Mum for taking me in and raising me as her own. This is a perfect example of our beautiful culture and kinship systems. There are many Aboriginal families who naturally come together and support each other, and it's not uncommon for our kids to be raised by aunts and uncles or grandparents.

Deadly Little Mumma

I was born with a maternal nature. I adore kids. I used to babysit a lot when I was younger. I had a deep sense of love and responsibility for my niece and nephews. I would babysit other kids from my flats too. I remember being young, maybe 11 or 12, and I was already babysitting two year olds. I was always an excellent little negotiator and would use these opportunities to make money, usually around 20 bucks; however, I was known to babysit for a TV and a wardrobe once, too.

I became a mother at 19 and have raised two beautiful children. I was in a happy relationship with the father of my children; an incredible man who was my first true love. After overcoming so much in my younger years, my life was complete. We were both working hard and raising our beautiful children.

I remember meeting Richard after a big night out clubbing with my beautiful sista, Kelly. We were at an early opener pub, still drinking and playing pool. I looked over and saw the future father of my children looking over at me.

It was love at first sight, and within a few months, I was pregnant with our son.

We spent the next eight years together, building a family and a home for our beautiful children, who were our pride and joy. Richard and I had an incredible relationship. He was an amazing father who loved our kids more than anything in this world. We seemed to have it all together.

For the first two years of Tyrell's life, I was a stay-at-home mum and Richard was a hard-working scaffolder. When Tyrell was two, I embarked on a career at St George Bank where I excelled at my job and was quickly promoted into a specialist position.

On the weekends, we would take our kids to football and athletics and enjoyed attending family events. Life was good.

When the Waves Came Crashing Down

Eight years after our relationship started, Richard passed away suddenly and very unexpectedly. I'm not going to go into too much about his passing out of respect for my children and his family as I am simply sharing my story of resilience and hope. Richard was an incredible man who lit up every room. He was kind, generous, caring and compassionate and would do anything for anyone.

After all the early years of struggle, my life was finally moving in the right direction. His passing can only be described as a severe stab in the heart. The shock and grief that I experienced during this time was unimaginable.

Losing Richard almost claimed my life too.

Just when I thought that God and the Universe would give me a break from all this grief and suffering, just two years after Rich passed away, Mum told me she'd been diagnosed with cancer. This news brought me to my knees and had me screaming to the heavens above, asking why these horrible things kept happening.

I couldn't help but wonder if I had been cursed.

I was absolutely shattered as Mum was my biggest support, and I didn't know how I would survive without her.

I did what I do best and showed up with care and compassion, full of love and kindness, and did my part in supporting Mum through the next two years of her battle with cancer until sadly, she passed away in 2011.

It is a time of great sadness that still sits heavy in my heart.

You really don't know how strong you are until you have no other choice than to be strong. There are so many times that I wanted to give up. The fear and grief were overwhelming at times. But through prayer and hope, I decided to wake up, count my blessings and move forward, one step at a time. One word that people often use to describe me is resilient – someone who has the ability to bounce back from adversity and challenges. My life has not been easy; however, I am someone who has a very strong spirit.

I am continuously being guided by my ancestors and my beautiful angels who are still with me every day.

Despite all of the challenges that I have experienced, I'm very proud to be here today and to be sharing my story, one of strength and perseverance. I share my journey purely to encourage others to never give up. As long as the sun is setting and rising again the next day, there is always hope.

We are the creators of our destiny and the captains of our ship.

I refuse to let circumstances dictate my future.

Where I Am Today

As I write this book, I am a happily married 40 year old woman. My incredible husband, Jamie, and I were married in 2015. He was a blessing in disguise, and together, we have created a life beyond what each of us could have ever imagined.

His upbringing was similar to mine; he grew up not having much. Jamie grew up in New Zealand and is proud of his Maori heritage. He is the most patient, kind and compassionate man I have ever met. I prayed for him, and he was sent my way. I am extremely grateful for our Maori whanau who are beyond incredible. They accepted me and the kids into their big and loving family. I express gratitude every day for the opportunity to experience happiness again – something I didn't ever think was possible.

My children know how lucky they are and will never take their experiences for granted. I have always instilled a sense of gratitude in them.

Tyrell was born a wise soul.

He has all the qualities any mother could ask for – kind, caring and compassionate. Tyrell truly is one of the most intelligent people I have ever met. He cares deeply for others and naturally makes all the right choices. Tyrell has made my job as his mother so easy. He's a bit like me when I was growing up, quiet with others and often crazy at home.

I remember the moment he was born as if it were yesterday. He had a full head of hair, and instantly, I fell in love. I remember his cute little voice and the way he used to touch my face as he fell asleep. He has always had a kind and gentle nature, always there to help anyone in need.

All of the kids in our life love Tyrell.

He is popular with the students at his work, where he is an Aboriginal Education Officer. At seven years old, he held my hand at his dad's funeral and has been my go-to man and support with all the major life decisions I have made. He has been my source of strength all these years, and he proudly walked me down the sandy aisle to marry my incredible husband, Jamie.

I am beyond blessed and extremely grateful for my amazing son.

Allira is the most incredible daughter.

Just like her brother and me, she is completing her HSC. Being an educator, this makes me so proud. Allira is my BFF and mini-me. Everyone says she's the *"spitting image"* of me.

Allira is a kind and gentle spirit. She is an amazing dancer and an incredible role model for the younger kids in our family and community. What I love most about my beautiful daughter is her big heart and her love of kids. She is smart and creative and has grown into a humble and reflective young lady with a crazy sense of humour that brings so much joy to my life.

It's sometimes like watching myself grow up all over again, except this time, I'm there to guide her on a path of positivity and give her every opportunity her heart desires. When I found out I was pregnant for the second time, I was ecstatic to hear that I was having a girl. I went in for a few more ultrasounds just to double – and triple – check.

My dream of having a daughter had come true.

She truly is the most incredible daughter who fills my heart with pride. I thank God every day for my beautiful girl.

I am grateful for all of my experiences, the good and the bad. All of the challenges as well as the tremendous success I have had.

I was the first in my family to complete a university degree whilst working full time and raising my two children. I am a homeowner and have bought my dream house here in Sydney. I have travelled to places some could only dream of, such as The Bahamas, Greece, Canada, Miami, Orlando, Los Angeles, Thailand, Bali, New Zealand, Fiji, Key West, Las Vegas and have even landed in the Grand Canyon by helicopter for lunch. My dream to take my kids to Disneyland came true in 2018. We left for a month-long trip around the States the day after my son graduated from his HSC.

I wanted to give my kids everything I didn't have. Not to spoil them but for my own sense of achievement – knowing that I made it.

> "Owning our story and loving ourselves through that process is the bravest thing we'll ever do."
> (Brené Brown)

Kylie with birth Mum Millie

We All Have a Story

Kylie with Mum Denise at the Tamworth Country Music Festival

Kylie as a baby with Mum Denise

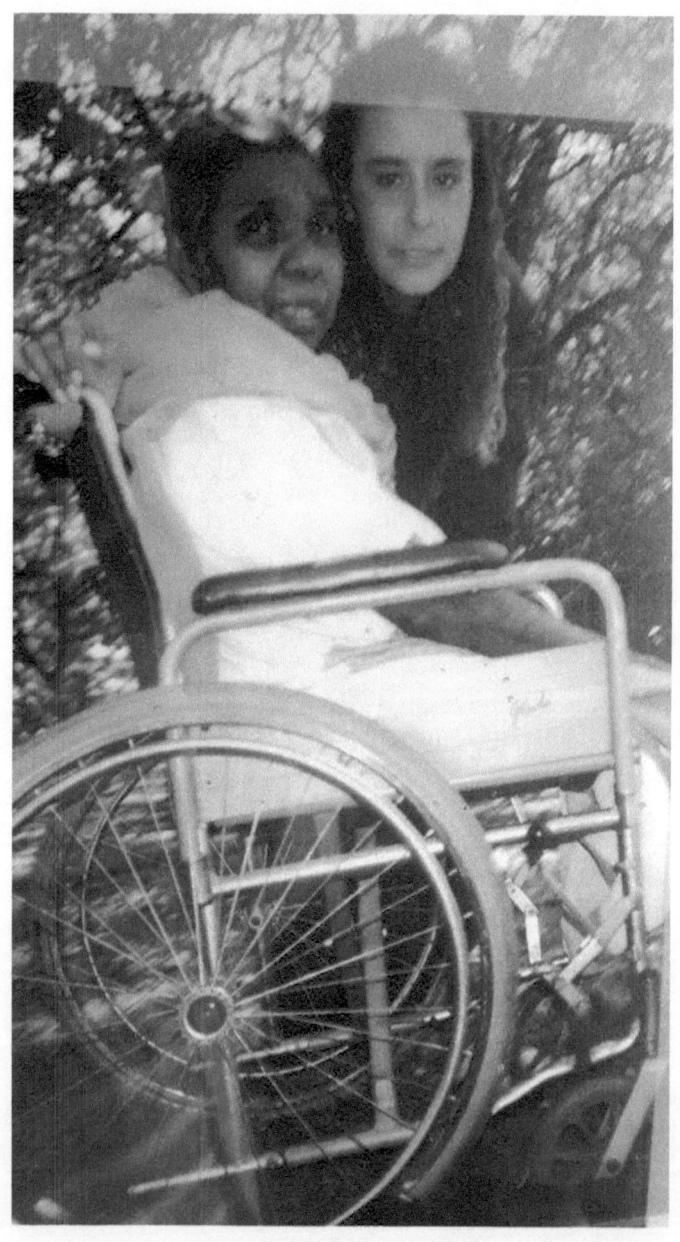

Kylie with Nan Delphine

Kylie with niece Kira as a baby

Kylie with sister Narelle and friend Diane

DREAM BIG & Imagine the What If

Kylie with dad Mick, Christmas 1985

We All Have a Story

Kylie as a child

Kylie as a student at Redfern Public School

Kylie with best friend Johanna at the Tamworth Country Music Festival

Kylie with sister Narelle and Nephew Trent

We All Have a Story

Kylie with Mum Denise on her 18th Birthday

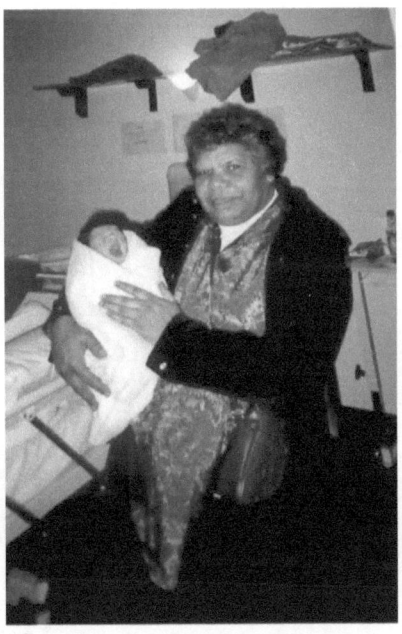

Mum Denise with Tyrell as a newborn

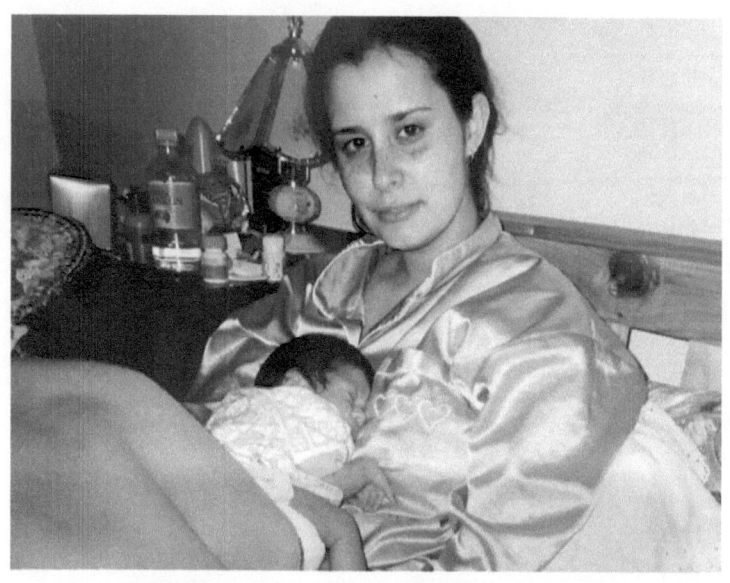

Kylie as a young mum with son Tyrell

Chapter Two

RIDING THE WAVES OF GRIEF

Grief is something that comes into your life and turns your world upside down in an instant. We never see it coming, and it often can be the experience that stops us in our tracks and destroys any hopes and dreams for the future. Many people never recover from grief; however, with understanding and the right support, I believe there is hope for everyone who may encounter such sadness.

Grief isn't always due to the death of a loved one. It can be from a breakdown in a relationship, a traumatic experience or even the loss of a pet. The grief we experience when we lose something or someone we love can be overwhelming and often send us into a spiral of shock, denial and numbness while at the same time, our mind and body works hard to process what is happening.

Psychiatrist Elizabeth Kübler-Ross explains the five stages of grief being: denial, anger, bargaining, sadness and acceptance. I have learnt to understand these stages and how they are all connected. I'll share my experience with some of these stages as everyone's experience with grief will be different, and you may not experience all of the stages outlined by experts.

Kübler-Ross explains that the first stage of grief is denial. This most certainly was my experience. Many people hope that they will wake up from a terrible dream when grief comes knocking at the door. This is when you are first faced with immediate shock and disbelief about the situation you're in. You may find yourself hoping and praying that you'll wake up from this terrible nightmare. You may feel numb and in disbelief; however, you soon realise that what you are experiencing is real. This stage is usually only short because adrenaline starts to kick in, and you're in fight or flight mode. Once the numbness wears off, all of the emotions of hurt, anger and incredible sadness set in, and you start on the rollercoaster journey of fighting and riding the inevitable waves of grief.

From my experience, anger usually comes next. This particular moment in time can be extremely intense and stir emotions and responses that you didn't know were possible. This is usually the point where you may find yourself screaming out for help and wondering, *"Why me?"*

Well, I know this was the case for me. You feel like the world is ganging up on you, and you wonder why God or whatever it is that you believe in has picked you to go through this devastating loss. You are purely in survival mode at this stage.

There comes a time during the process when you start to have hope. The fighter within you begins to kick in, and you have this incredible energy to regain control and recreate some sort of normality within your life.

Sadness and depression often set in when going through the stages of grief, which we as a society don't talk about enough. After trying to be hopeful, sometimes you get to the point where it doesn't matter how positive and optimistic you are; you come to realise that what you are doing isn't working or happening fast enough. This stage of depression may cause you to feel vulnerable and tired and not want to participate in events or things you previously did. This is a challenging stage because the feeling of depression and sadness is often the hardest one to pull yourself out of.

Acceptance is a stage that usually follows after depression. Once you've hit rock bottom, there is no other way than up, so you start to accept your situation and try to learn new ways to re-adjust to life. At this stage, you may begin to try to surround yourself with family and loved ones and may be able to start to talk about the event to some degree without it causing you to spiral back into the depression stage. Acceptance is all about understanding that what you're going through won't disappear, however knowing that there is no way out apart from taking those first steps towards a brighter future.

My advice for anyone who is experiencing grief is to visualise yourself sailing on a ship. Know that the waves will sometimes become rough and knock you down; however, there are always smoother seas ahead. Keep moving forward, one step at a time. Know that it doesn't matter how rough the seas may get, there is always hope that the next day will present calmer seas for you to enjoy the smooth sailing.

Later, I'll share strategies and suggestions that helped me and may help others, too.

Remember that God, the Universe or any higher power you may or may not believe in will only send you challenges and experiences they think you can handle. I always look at these challenges as life assignments. It's like we're being tested to see if we can survive and get through. For what reason, I don't know.

All I know is that life is one big test, and sometimes it's not about how well you do; it's just about passing.

In August of 2007, when Richard tragically passed away, I was broken. I went from being part of a happy family with hopes and dreams for the future to a single mum of two children aged just three and seven years old. I had no idea how or whether I would survive that time in my life. All the good in my life was ripped from beneath me. My world was turned upside down. The trauma of this experience almost killed me; however, it also shaped me into the strong, resilient woman I am today.

He is still with us in spirit and I see him in my children every day. I remember the moment I saw Rich for the first time.

Such a kind and gentle spirit. I honestly feel that I fell instantly in love with him.

When we met, I was shy and insecure. I had suffered from psoriasis most of my life. I would drink and take drugs to numb what I was feeling. I was often ashamed and embarrassed because of my skin. I never thought anyone would love me, and I never thought anyone would see past the scales on my skin and see me for who I really was.

I thought it would only be a matter of time before he saw my skin and would be disgusted and would move on – but he didn't. The love we had was real, it was pure and it was true.

I remember looking back at photos and seeing my psoriasis. Most of the time I would avoid the camera. Richard never even noticed my skin; well, I'm sure he did, but he never let me know it. I have tears flowing down my face as I write and reflect on just how special this amazing man was. He changed my life in so many ways. He blessed me with my beautiful children and showed me the true meaning of love. We laughed, we cried and enjoyed the most incredible eight years together. He was an amazing father who I know continues to guide and protect us.

I was in total shock and disbelief about the fact he was gone. At just 30 years of age, he still had his whole life ahead of him.

I was in survival mode.

I had to protect myself from the triggers and memories I didn't want to see every day, so the first decision I made was to move out of our family home. I didn't know where we were going, but I started packing our things. After a few moves that didn't work out, I was fortunate enough to have my good friends, Karen and Shane, come to our aid and offer for me and the kids to stay with them.

I found it hard to believe how life could change overnight. We had a beautiful home, great jobs, and healthy, happy children. Waking up to life as a single mother broke my heart into a million pieces. It truly was the worst pain I have ever experienced. It still brings up so much sadness when I think of this time in my life.

It is a pain that no one should have to experience.

I did my absolute best to be strong in front of my kids as I saw their innocence in all that was happening. They didn't want to see me sad. I felt their love and compassion as they looked at me, saying, *"Are you okay, Mumma?"*

We slept in the same bed together, and I held them tight every night, praying for strength and guidance. I was terrified about what the future held. I wasn't prepared to do life on my own. I remember crying myself to sleep each night, in shock at where my life had ended up. After all that hard work to overcome the challenges of my younger years, I now had to face life as a single mum and sadly watch my kids grow up without the love of a parent, a pain and sadness I knew too well. Every time I looked at my babies, my heart broke.

The grief I experienced was unimaginable.

I had no goals or aspirations, and I really did feel like my life was over. We were living day by day and week by week, simply trying to survive. I put on a brave face; however, deep down, I was terrified about what the future held for us.

Each day was filled with tears. I did my best to hide them from my kids and work colleagues, but sometimes it was just too hard. I would break down and sob uncontrollably. Simple things like taking my kids to the park or grocery shopping were difficult as I would look at the other families and be devastated about where we had ended up. I would cry myself to sleep and when alone, I would scream at God for putting us in that situation.

I didn't want to live; it was too hard.

The thought crossed my mind about ending it. I feel absolutely ashamed to say it, but that's how deeply depressed I felt at the time. When I looked at my beautiful, innocent children, I would think, *"What about them? Who would look after them? No one could love them the way I do."*

I didn't see any hope or happiness for us in the future.

I quickly sent myself into a panic and started to shift my thoughts and closed my eyes and started to dream. I would imagine seeing my kids smiling, running, swimming and playing, all the things any mother wants for her children. I started to visualise myself there with them; this gave me hope.

I'll never forget Richard. He truly was the most incredible man and father.

When you've experienced as much grief as I have, you'll know that it's a few months later when everything hits you. When all the support drops off and everyone around you forgets the initial shock. The check-in calls often slow down and you really start to feel alone.

Our first Christmas without him was the hardest. The friends we were staying with went to New Zealand for a holiday, so it was just me and the kids at home. I was dreading Christmas; however, I had two little children who deserved all the joy that Christmas brings. I felt alone, and I didn't want us to be on our own for Christmas.

I decided to book a holiday to the Gold Coast. It was tough, but I did my best. My cousin, Damien, and his wife, Fani, drove up to be with us so we weren't alone. Whilst it was a great time visiting theme parks and enjoying summer by the pool, deep down, I was lost. I remember my cousin looking at me; I could feel his empathy.

He went on to say, *"I know you don't want to hear this right now, but you will have a great future and you will love again."*

I actually wanted to scream and burst into tears as I thought there was no way I was ever going to love again, and I most certainly didn't see a great future ahead. I smiled and politely thanked him for being there with us which made the world of difference.

As I progressed through the stages of grief, I remember thinking, *"What if? What if the kids and I could go on to have a good life and a decent future despite what we were experiencing?"*

I closed my eyes and would create movies in my mind about the life I wanted.

I would bring myself to tears of happiness just thinking about being happy. I wished I could stay in this dream forever because whenever I opened my eyes, I was reminded of the heartbreaking situation we were in.

Our friends so generously allowed us to stay until I felt strong enough to start again on my own. We stayed for six months until one day I just said, *"I'm ready."*

I was a woman on a mission – I would not let our circumstances ruin the lives of my babies.

All that praying and dreaming was starting to work. I could visualise a happy future for us, and I was about to do everything in my power to make it happen.

We moved into a rental and started to take life head-on. It was hard; my goal was just to get through each day. Grief is something you will never get over; you simply learn to ride the waves and deal with it. Sometimes the waves will get rough and knock you down; however, you know sooner or later, there will be calmer seas ahead.

From this time, the seas continued to become rough. Just two years after losing Richard, Mum was diagnosed with cancer. That was like another kick in the guts. The whole cycle of grief continued, a feeling I was almost getting used to. Fortunately, she survived two years after her diagnosis, and we managed to spend so many incredible moments with her.

As time went on, I started to set goals and dream of the things I hoped to achieve in life. The thought crossed my mind about the possibility of buying my own home. I was very good with money and had been saving as much as I could.

I had a permanent job and had worked continuously for the past eight years, so my credit file was relatively healthy. I would write down all of my income and expenditure and tried to budget as best I could. I wasn't into spending on big brands and I had this burning desire to be a customer of the bank I once worked in; however, this time, I wanted to be on the other side of the counter applying for a home loan. This was something I knew was almost impossible; however, I wanted to challenge myself to see if this impossible dream could become a reality.

Break up the word impossible, and it says 'I'm-possible' – and that is what I started to believe.

I set out on a mission to buy my own home. I became obsessed with researching the market. I was always on real estate websites and became familiar with the going prices for homes. In 2009, I was eager to speak with a home loan lender to ask about the borrowing process and have my finances reviewed to one day be applying for a home loan.

I arranged a meeting with a lender at the bank where I once worked. I remember being very nervous and excited, praying and praying for guidance and direction.

After deep consideration of my circumstances, I was approved for a home loan.

I couldn't believe it. It seriously was one of the most terrifying things I have ever done, leaving the security of community housing to set out on a new adventure as a single mum and buying my first home.

I'm proud to say that after all the grief and hard moments, in 2009, I purchased my first property and AS A SINGLE MUM! I'm still super proud of myself for this achievement. Mum was still alive at this stage, and I can still see her face and hear her voice telling me how proud she was as I took her on a tour of our new home.

This was one of the greatest moments in my life.

From there, I started to realise my potential and knew I could do anything I set my mind to.

I have survived, and I am incredibly proud of my attitude towards life and my ability to make the right choices when things get tough. I am forever grateful for my children, who are my reason for living, and the faces I focused on through all the grief I experienced.

I've been through all the stages of grief and would never wish that pain upon anyone. The sad truth is that everyone will experience it at some point, and I hope the information and strategies shared in this chapter and later in the book will help others ride the waves and sail through to the calmer seas ahead.

*"Nothing is impossible,
the word itself says 'I'm possible'!"
(Audrey Hepburn)*

Kylie, Richard, Tyrell and Allira

Kylie, Richard and Tyrell

Kylie, Richard and Allira

DREAM BIG & Imagine the What If

Tyrell and Allira at Movie World, their first Christmas after Richard passed away.

Chapter Three

BLACK AND PROUD

My Aboriginality has always been something I've been so proud of. From a very young age, my culture has made me feel strong and formed my identity. The connections, the laughs, the yarns with my mob and other blackfullas keeps me grounded.

Being Aboriginal is hard to describe. It comes from within.

It's like this warm fuzzy feeling that sits deep inside my chest. I think it's my ancestors keeping me safe and forever guiding and protecting my journey. Knowing that I come from a culture that is the longest-living surviving culture in the world, where resilience is a legacy of generations of ancestors who are so smart and deadly, fills my heart with pride.

If Mum didn't take me and raise me as her own after Mum Millie passed, I could have missed out on growing up black. Fortunately for me, a big part of our culture is the importance of kinship and looking after each other. I don't think Mum thought twice about taking me, it was something I feel just happened naturally. She became my mum, and her three daughters became my sisters. Everyone in our community knew that Mum was my mum and my sisters were my sisters – not my cousins.

I dedicate my life and career to enhancing a system that ensures Aboriginal students have access to a quality education, where their culture is valued and celebrated. For far too long, our people have not engaged – not because they don't value education – but because the past injustices have made it difficult to do so.

Past policies and the mistreatment of my people have severed the trust in many of the systems in this country.

Countless numbers of my people were denied an education simply because they were Aboriginal.

I remember Mum telling me that she had to go and work for white people on cattle stations as a domestic servant when she was 11. Back then, there was an exclusion on demand policy where for any given reason, any Aboriginal child could be denied an education.

Mum was born in 1952 and wasn't a citizen in this country until she was 15 years old when 90 percent of Australians voted to count Aboriginal people in the Census.

Mum lived in Walgett, a small rural town in North West New South Wales, where she experienced the horrific segregation and discrimination that was common, right across this great country.

Aboriginal people weren't allowed in pools, pubs, theatres and at times, even schools. No wonder Mum had such a big issue with white people. Even though she never had nice things to say about them, she would always encourage me to go to school and say things like, *"You go Kylie, you know how to talk to them whitefullas."*

I would tell her that they weren't all bad and share stories about some deadly teachers and white people who I knew were doing good things for our people. I believe this helped break down some of the barriers.

Connecting to Country Is Good for the Soul

Connecting to Country is more than just a connection to a place. It's the stories, family, culture and relationships that form our identity and who we are as Aboriginal people.

The connection is hard to describe. It's a feeling of peace and a place that just feels right. We all have those special places that bring us an overwhelming sense of comfort. Whether it's being out in nature or by the sea, the feeling of Connecting to Country Is Good for the Soul.

As a child, I loved travelling back to Walgett. I was always so excited to see my beautiful Nan, Kathleen Boney, who we knew as Nanna KB. She was always so happy to see us and made us feel so welcome in her home.

I always felt a sense of freedom in Walgett. It felt like a weight had been lifted off my shoulders. Getting out of the city and breathing in the fresh country air was soothing.

I loved lying in Nanna KB's backyard at night. Me and my cousins would lay on the trampoline and stare up at the stars. The stillness in the air was magical. The sky pitch black and the stars so bright.

It was easy to allow the mind to wander and think of all of our old people who had gone before us. Their stories, their struggles and their resilience, all whose legacy lives on in our hearts and minds.

Even though I wasn't born in Walgett, I have always felt a deep connection to this place. The Country that Mum Millie and Mum Denise were born and raised on and called home. The stories of their upbringing, playing by the river and levy bank are etched in my memory forever.

The smell of the freshness in the air is something I often long for.

I still love to visit Walgett and have made a point over the last few years to get there for things other than funerals. I love seeing my beautiful Aunt Diane, who is like a mother to me. She is always so kind and generous with her yarns, where she shares stories about her life growing up by the river with Mum Millie and Mum Denise. They grew up like siblings, and I'm thankful to still have my Aunt Di in my life.

I loved roaming around and playing with my cousins over the river. Bingo was a hit. There was always good money to be won. Sometimes Mum would let me play. There was something therapeutic about sitting on the ground and using dirt to cover the numbers on the wooden bingo cards.

I wanted to live in Walgett in my early teens. Mum allowed me to travel there many times during the holidays. I stayed with my Aunt Violet as I loved spending time with my cousin Deanna. One of my favourite Christmases was in Walgett when Aunt Violet bought me and Deanna cameras. We thought we were so deadly.

My family have always had a special bond with our Boney mob, some who have now passed. My deadly Uncle Darce, Uncle Arch, Aunt Nina, Aunt Violet, Aunt Diane and aunty Heather were like mothers and fathers to me and my sisters.

One of my favourite trips was when Uncle Arch travelled with me and my sister on the train and bus to get there. The excitement would always kick in when we reached Coonamble as I knew there was only about an hour to go.

There is so much beauty in Country. Staring out as far as the eye can see is a feeling that fills my spirit with the comfort and the ongoing healing it needs.

I remember feeling a little disconnected a few years ago, and my reiki therapist, Mel, told me I should go to the river. She is very intuitive and has been a source of healing and guidance over the years. It was the school holidays, so the following morning, I packed some things into the car, and the kids and I made the nine-hour drive to Walgett. It just felt right.

When we arrived, Aunt Diane had lots of old photos of Mum Millie and Mum Denise that I hadn't seen before and she was keen to take us over the river to show us exactly where they lived.

The remains of their old tin shack were still there. As we sat and reminisced, Tyrell started to wander off into the bush. He returned about 15 minutes later, telling us that he had found a plaque with photos and stories with information about Nan and other local people. Aunt Diane or my cousins didn't even know those plaques existed.

We were meant to go to the river that day, and Tyrell was meant to stumble across those plaques.

There were stories about Nan marrying a local Chinese man named Lenny Chong who worked in the 'Chinamen Gardens'. I don't know if that yarn is true. The stories spoke of the respectful relationship between workers in the Chinamen Gardens and the local Aboriginal community. They shared fruit and vegetables in return for local knowledge to help grow their crops. I couldn't help but laugh as Nan always told me that Lenny Chong was my grandfather.

I don't know if that yarn is true either.

We returned home feeling refreshed and revitalised. The disconnect I was feeling had been restored. My spirit was uplifted and I was ready to return to our busy life in Sydney.

In my teens, I begged Mum to let me live there with Aunt Violet. I didn't want to go back to the city; however, it wasn't long before Mum would show up, telling me to get home.

I remember being over the river (Namoi Reserve) and feeling so excited to see my Uncle Son Boy come back from the cattle station he was working at. He had a sheep with him, which I thought was so cute. Unfortunately, this memory soon turned into a horror story as he proceeded to cut the sheep's throat right there in front of us. That poor sheep was our dinner for the next few weeks. I found it hard to eat it. I'm lucky that experience didn't turn me off meat altogether.

A special man in my life has been my Uncle Arch.

Sadly, we lost him a few years ago. He was on a pension; however, he was the person to buy me my first mobile phone. It was a Nokia 6110 with interchangeable covers. He didn't have much money; however, was always so generous to me. He promised he would buy me the phone on pension day, and he never failed to follow through with his promises. I remember that day as it felt like all of my Christmases had come at once. We walked up to the Redfern Street Hock Shop and bought the phone that I had my eye on. I thought I was so deadly with my new phone.

I've always been so grateful to Uncle Arch for his generosity.

When Uncle Arch got sick, we knew he didn't have much time. I helped him pack up his things from his little unit in Sydney as he knew it was time to go home. He came and spent one last night with us, and I made him a lovely chicken soup.

He travelled home to Walgett the following day and a few months later, he was gone. I remember talking to him on the phone and telling him I was coming to see him as we knew he didn't have much time. I told him the date that I would be there as school holidays were approaching. Thankfully, he held on until we got there so we could see him one last time. After we left the hospital, it wasn't long before Aunt Diane called to say he was gone.

Uncle Arch was a man of few words; however, when he spoke, you listened deeply as his kindness and love for his people filled your spirit with pure joy.

The kids and I miss our dear uncle every day.

Be the Change You Want to See

I work in Aboriginal-identified positions in the hope to be an advocate and changemaker for my people. What saddens me most about being Australian is that our history has been swept under the rug, and our voices silenced so our stories have not been heard.

I embarked on a career in education because I feel it's where I can have the most impact. Gaining an education has the ability to change the trajectory of someone's life. It offers freedom and choice, something everyone should have. It was a few kind teachers who made a difference for me, so I think it's fitting that I pay it forward and do the same for other Aboriginal students.

Many things can be taken from you, but no one can take away what you have learnt. Education is a right, and we know it changes lives.

Our kids deserve a quality education where their culture is embedded into curriculum so that they feel like they don't have to continuously live in two worlds.

I love my job, and I'm pretty deadly at it. I am a proud and passionate educator, making a difference for our students, families and communities. I trained as a primary school teacher, and now I support teachers and principals to implement an inclusive curriculum by encouraging truth-telling and building relationships with Aboriginal students, families and communities.

I share my knowledge and experience with educators in order for them to build empathy and understanding. Some teachers and leaders I work with sometimes need to learn, re-learn or un-learn the truth about our incredible country.

Many have missed out on the opportunity to learn the truth of our history, and once they do, are often keen to join our journey of change.

Australia is an extremely diverse country with many language groups, clans and nations; therefore, the stories and experiences from each group are different. I don't claim to be an expert on the diversity or stories of the many peoples, cultures and languages across Australia and the Torres Strait Islands. I just know that things have not been done right in this country. I do my best to try to explain this through my story, experiences and the things I've learnt.

Always Was, Always Will Be

Prior to invasion, there were more than 500 Aboriginal Nations spread right across Australia. These nations had been here for 65,000+ years, making Aboriginal people the longest-living surviving culture in the world – pretty deadly hey! This is something to be so proud of.

I always tell our young people to be proud of their Aboriginality, as we are the smartest and deadliest humans on the planet.

Our knowledge systems and ability to think creatively and innovatively, and therefore, survive this long is incredible. We were the first engineers, the first scientists, and the first to establish sophisticated societies in harmony with the environment. Every member of the community was responsible for caring for the land and ensuring that it was maintained with resources sustained.

These reciprocal obligations ensured our survival for tens of thousands of generations.

Aboriginal peoples across the many nations have always had an intimate relationship with the land, seas and skies. The Acknowledgement of and Welcome to Country is evidence of this. They would not step onto new land without being invited or welcomed.

They would always acknowledge the Traditional Custodians of the land and thank them for allowing them to pass through or obtain resources. This ceremony would protect the owners of Country, as well as those visiting or simply passing through.

Each clan and language group has their own beliefs, language, customs, Dreaming, and creation stories, and their own laws and lores.

Australia's history is complex, contested and violent, and not one to be proud of.

I believe, however, that through education that listens to and respects our voices, we can come to a place of healing and perhaps, true reconciliation. We need to acknowledge the past and recognise our shared histories, in order to move forward with positivity and hope for a brighter future.

Since the arrival of the British and up until the late twentieth century, many of my people were forbidden to speak their language. This resulted in a devastating loss of culture and identity, particularly in the southeastern states which were the first to feel the effects of dispossession and white man's hunger for land. For anyone who is part of a thriving culture or community, it is incredibly difficult to imagine how devastating this loss would be.

We must remember that Australia since invasion is still a very new country. Policies that have been implemented across this land have been deliberately discriminatory, often violent and always punishing; a true embarrassment to the governments who implemented them.

These horrific policies resulted in the mixing of language groups, undermining Aboriginal people's sophisticated social, political and legal structures. There were kinship systems regarding who you could marry, what responsibilities you had within the community, and the resources and totems you were responsible for.

The rounding up of my people, placing them on missions and reserves, took away their control, dignity and therefore, humanity.

The sense of responsibility to care for their land to carry out all that was required of them was ripped from beneath them, leaving them purposeless and powerless.

My people were forbidden to access traditional medicines and foods and forced to live off rations such as flour and sugar. The control of and the ability to live a self-sufficient life was taken. Those who refused to live by these new rules experienced the full force of the law and the consequences of not conforming was violence, torture and imprisonment, often followed by premature death.

We can't deny the fact that there were massacres which led to severe depression and sadness that is still evident in the lives of many today.

Intergenerational Trauma is Real

My great-grandmother, Elsie Captain (nee Boman), passed away in January of 1937, aged just 20 years. The cause of death identified on her death certificate is 'tuberculosis and suicide by cut throat.'

This saddens me as perhaps if she had freedom and access to traditional medicines, she would have survived longer than her short 20 years. The fact that she took her own life demonstrates the true despair and agony she experienced. Like many introduced diseases, tuberculosis was one that caused a significant death toll among Aboriginal people, which also fed into the idea that Aboriginal people were a dying race.

My grandmother, Delphine Captain, was three years old at the time of Nan Elsie's death. My great-grandfather, Roland Captain, also known as Roly Captain Winton, was a tracker attached to Roma Police Station in Queensland. The historical police records show he continuously requested dismissal from his role. I hear he was a clever man so no wonder the police wanted him to work for them. From my research, I feel he was very unhappy, perhaps from the burden he carried as a servant to white people.

After many attempts and leaving without approval, he was finally granted a leave of absence to return to Worrabinda, located in Central Queensland. According to the records, he 'became very unsettled and discontented' before leaving. He expressed his desire to return home to be with his wife and daughter. He intended on travelling on a bike in the rain. While a journey like that today takes five hours on a bitumen road, you can only imagine how long his journey would have taken him back then.

The police had many failed attempts to induce him to return.

I reflect on the treatment and experience of my great-grandparents and can't help but feel sad. Nan was lucky to survive, as Central Queensland had a high level of frontier violence and Aboriginal deaths. Dispossessed survivors were forced into government-controlled settlements and with the introduction of the Aborigines Protection Act, it's reported that Aboriginal Peoples from many different language groups were said to be placed in Woorabinda and were under the control of a local Chief Protector of Aborigines.

When Nan was six, Grandfather Roly passed away, so she was cared for by a grandfather who took her to Walgett where the rest of her mob was. Nan then spent her childhood and adult years living in Walgett where she had her two daughters, my beautiful mothers – Denise and Millie.

These stories, supported by research findings, show that intergenerational trauma is evident within many Aboriginal families. They say it takes about six generations to wipe out this trauma, even when people were not directly affected. This is seen in the lives of many around us.

Too many people feel and think that our people should 'just get over it'.

I'm here to say that we can't just get over it, just like no one would expect any other family to get over a traumatic event in their family history. The trauma is still evident in the gaps that we see in society today.

Closing the Educational Gap

The gaps between Aboriginal and non-Aboriginal student achievement in school tells us that there is still so much work to be done. Many of our young people are still not finishing school or going on to further education. Some feel their history and culture is not valued at school. Research studies and anecdotal data shows that many of our young people feel that they need to leave their culture at the door when they enter the school gates and so the assimilatory effects of schooling continue.

Schools are still scary places for a lot of our people, so it is sometimes difficult to come into a school to talk about their children and their education. For some of our parents and grandparents, they see these government schools as a threat because of past government policies that removed their children and excluded them from education.

This is their experience, this is their fear, and it is real. Many don't trust the systems or the people who work in them.

I don't have the answers on how to fix these issues; however, from my experience, there is so much that can be done to start the process of healing and true reconciliation. I feel that introducing culturally safe practices that explicitly value and hear the voices of our families is a great place to start. Families need to feel they can be involved in and contribute to their child's education. Our people are smart and have a lot to offer, but this has to be done through a long process of building relationships and trust.

My dream is that we'll see improved educational outcomes and more Aboriginal students will recognise their potential, believe in themselves and chase their dreams.

The Pain and Heartache Still Fresh in the Hearts and Minds of Many

The devastating historical mistreatment of Aboriginal people is still fresh in the hearts and minds of many. Many children were stolen from their families. They were institutionalised and trained for domestic and farm labour. There was no reason for this other than to breed the black out of them and prop up the economy with free labour. There were policies in place that removed Aboriginal children from their families for any or even no reason. Many of our people grew up in these homes and institutions they were placed in, sometimes as young as babies. They were stripped of their name and often told that their families had either died or didn't want them anymore.

Many of the survivors talk about their experience and how they were abused and brainwashed. They were denied the opportunity to grow up with their families and communities where they were loved and looked after. Instead, they grew up in homes where they were often subject to physical, sexual and mental abuse; trauma which affects not only them but their children and their children's children.

These horrific policies resulted in a loss of spirit, loss of culture and the destruction of our kinship systems. Many Aboriginal people who were part of the Stolen Generations never found their way home.

Those who managed to make their way back to their families and communities often found that life was never the same, as while they were away, they were forced to think and act white. To understand this, you need to listen to the words of Uncle

Archie Roach's song, *Took the Children Away*.

I encourage every Australian to reflect on his words, listen to the meaning, listen to Uncle's experience – it is heartbreaking.

Talking about this stuff breaks my heart and brings me to tears.

It affects my spirit, it affects who I am, and it is not right. I feel it's a must for all Australians to know. I want everyone to know because I'm sick of my people being stereotyped. I don't want my nieces and nephews and communities to have to always defend themselves or to be judged because they are black.

Racism Still Exists in Australia

I have many examples I can share with you. I have nephews and nieces with dark skin and some who are fair. I absolutely love and adore all my babies and I want nothing more than for them to grow up feeling proud of who they are and not continuously experience discrimination because they are Aboriginal.

I remember being followed around a store by a security guard because I had my two beautiful black nephews with me – this made me furious. Self-control about how we respond to these events is important as I know no one will listen if I'm screaming and carrying on. I choose to educate politely and bring people along on the journey through building relationships and understanding. I point out their ugly attitudes by educating and encouraging empathy.

Racial profiling has been happening for far too long, and unfortunately, it's still happening today. Sadly, many Aboriginal people report being questioned or searched by police simply for walking down the street. Our prisons and Juvenile Justice Centres are full of our people. It's sad to think that statistics show that our young people are more likely to be locked up than they are to finish school.

I dream of a day when we're no longer having this yarn, when things are different for my people.

I think about my little brother Patrick Fisher and TJ Hickey, a young brother from my community who were reportedly chased to their deaths, being pursued by the police. Most recently, my nephew Gordon Copeland went missing. It's reported that he was last seen by police running into the Gwydir River outside the town of Moree. At the time of writing, Gordon has been missing for two months. The family and local community have been searching tirelessly with little resources or support to find him.

The trauma and sadness sit heavy in the hearts and minds of the devastated families and wider Aboriginal communities. Unfortunately, this trauma is passed on to future generations, and the cycle of intergenerational trauma continues.

Racial profiling and racist stereotypes that our people experience needs critical and urgent attention. I believe it starts with education and truth-telling.

Our Kids Need to Stay With Family

The Stolen Generations is another topic that continues to cause so much sadness in our communities.

When we reflect on The Apology and events like Sorry Day, one would think we are in a position to move forward with love and positivity whilst righting the wrongs of the past. However, the sad truth is the fact that Aboriginal kids are still overrepresented in the 'Out of Home Care' system.

Our kids need to stay with their families and communities.

Before pursuing a career in education, I worked with the Department of Communities and Justice as an early intervention caseworker. Being a carer for my 12 year old nephew at 21 taught me a lot about the 'system', and the lack of empathy and understanding these organisations had for Aboriginal families.

This motivated me to want to work for them as I thought that perhaps I could teach them a thing or two. I've always been someone who has wanted to do more and help where needed, believing I could make a difference. While I feel I did do that to some degree, this issue is bigger, broader and more complex, requiring critical and urgent attention from governments and their policy makers.

I reflect on my upbringing and how proud and connected I am to my culture, and I feel a deep sense of sadness for those who are stripped of this privilege which forms their identity and gives purpose, culture and connection.

It Doesn't Matter How Much Milk You Add – It's Still Tea

Blackfullas often use the analogy of a cup of tea. It doesn't matter how much milk you add - it's still tea.

Just because I have mixed blood, it doesn't make me less Aboriginal.

My father, Mick, is a white man whose people originate from Ireland and because I have fair skin, I'm often asked what ethnicity I am. Sometimes people are shocked when I say I'm Aboriginal.

I'm often told that I don't look Aboriginal and people sometimes ask, what percentage I am – which I find extremely offensive. As blackfullas, we don't go by what percentage we are. It's not about the colour of my skin, it's about the culture and the heritage that runs through my blood.

It's who I am.

We don't use terms such as half-caste or quarter-caste either. You're either Aboriginal or you're not. I continuously educate people about the fact that we come in all different shades and that it doesn't matter how black we are; it comes from within.

If I didn't have access to a mirror, I would think that I was just as black as my beautiful grandmother – and she was black! My culture and who I am runs deep within my soul.

There is a three-part definition about Aboriginality that we must satisfy when we apply for things like Aboriginal-identified jobs. It was created in the early 1980s by the Commonwealth Department of Aboriginal Affairs. The definition states an Aboriginal or Torres Strait Islander is a person of Aboriginal or Torres Strait Islander descent, who identifies as an Aboriginal or Torres Strait Islander and is accepted as such by the community in which he or she lives.

Aboriginal Land Councils may provide confirmation of Aboriginality if you satisfy the above requirements. As you can imagine, this is a sensitive topic, particularly for those who may have been part of the Stolen Generations – and for those who are just starting out on their journey of finding out who they are.

Identity

Identity is a topic that causes controversy and frustration in Aboriginal communities as many people find out they're Aboriginal and want to fast track their journey of identifying, hoping there may be some free government handouts – that ironically don't exist.

This is a stereotype where people think that blackfullas get everything for free. Today, income through means testing determines the government support people are entitled to, not ethnicity.

Some people choose to apply for Aboriginal-Identified jobs once they have their newfound culture. Those jobs that are there to support those who have the lived experiences and can be an authentic voice and role model for future generations.

Our culture and stories can't continue if the people telling the stories don't have the lived experience.

The struggles, the trauma, the pride in culture and resilience can't be learnt from a textbook.

There is a difference between having Aboriginal heritage and having the culture, history and stories ingrained in you. It's a sensitive topic, and I respect everyone's journey and encourage anyone who wants to explore their heritage to think about the reason they are doing it.

There are no free handouts as some may think; in fact, the sad truth is that what we do get is lower life expectancy, lower educational outcomes, along with higher rates of suicide, incarceration, child mortality, homelessness – as well as our kids over-represented in the Out of Home Care and Juvenile Justice Systems.

This is the sad reality for many of my people.

For those starting out on their journey, I encourage you to start with a yarn and respectfully explore your story and then discover who you are. There are incredible organisations to support this process, and I wish you nothing but love and strength as you go on your journey.

Education Is the Key

As a proud Aboriginal woman, I choose to work in education because I believe education changes lives. The impact and the work that I do reaches so many and I'm thankful for my non-Aboriginal colleagues who walk alongside us to bring about the much-needed education and change.

In my role, I encourage schools to focus on all of the significant people and events that have shaped Australia. We usually hear about the footy players and the actors and actresses. Don't get me wrong, these people need to be celebrated; however, I would love to see more everyday people being highlighted, too.

Our kids need to see success in their communities and when I say success, I mean in all different forms and examples of success. I also acknowledge that success comes in many different forms. Success isn't about how much money you make or about how many university degrees you have – it's about the contribution that you make.

When I was growing up, I didn't see many blackfullas highlighted as successful. I knew about the athletes and the footy players – I even went to school with some. However, I was never athletic, and I would've loved to have heard about the Aboriginal teachers, lawyers and authors.

I believe our kids need to see themselves in those they aspire to be.

There are so many significant people and events that can be highlighted in our communities, and I encourage schools to look at the Aboriginal calendar throughout the year and celebrate the deadly blackfullas in their communities.

Many Australians wouldn't know about significant events such as the Freedom Ride, the 1967 Referendum, the Mabo Decision and the National Apology.

Significant people who have made a difference for our people. Those brave people who stood up for what was right. It is because of them that I am here telling my story. People like Uncle Lyall Munro whose kids I grew up with. Uncle Lyall joined Charles Perkins Freedom Ride in 1965. They were protesting about the poor state of Aboriginal health, education and housing in western and coastal New South Wales. He also led a workers' strike at Wee Waa to protest against the $1 per hour wages.

People like Professor Bob Morgan, who I refer to as Uncle Bob, is a highly respected Aboriginal educator, researcher and social justice advocate who has worked extensively throughout Australia and internationally in the field of Aboriginal knowledge and learning for over 40 years.

There are so many incredible Aboriginal and Torres Strait Islander people who have worked tirelessly for equality and change.

The sad truth is that the media have focused their energy on the things that portray our people in a negative light.

It saddens me to think that our education system has failed so many.

If you're hearing these things for the first time, I encourage you to learn more – to read more and connect with Aboriginal people. Listen to the stories and experiences of local people in your community.

Reach out and get to know your community.

Ensure that they feel valued and build a relationship through trust and respect. Don't be afraid to ask questions and remember to listen and learn respectfully. Where you can, attend community events. One of my favourite events throughout the year is Survival Day on 26th January. For many Australians, this day is known as Australia Day.

Growing up, I didn't know that Australia Day and Survival Day were the same thing. I always remember celebrating Survival Day, where big mobs of our people would come together and celebrate the fact that we are still here. We celebrate because we have survived, despite the many challenges, policies and tragedies that were inflicted upon our families and communities.

For our teachers and leaders in our schools and communities, I encourage you to develop empathy and understanding about our history.

I encourage you to learn more and to do more to make a difference. I do not wish to place blame or make you feel guilty because our history is not your fault – we all know this. We need your empathy, understanding and support to move towards a brighter future where we can all be proud of our country. A country who understands its sad history and a country who recognises Aboriginal people; their knowledges, cultures and histories that have been here for tens of thousands of years.

Along with the sad history, there is the rich and beautiful culture that is there for all to learn more about and engage with.

The gaps that are still evident in the many reports these days are heartbreaking.

The number of suicides in our communities is devastating. The incarceration rates, number of deaths in custody, rates of mental illness, substance abuse and unemployment are heartbreaking. Though they are still part of our story, I'm hopeful this will change. The more we educate and build empathy and understanding to support healing from the trauma that we have collectively suffered, the more things will start to shift.

My people – I love you and I'm here for you.

There is nothing that makes me prouder than to see my people doing well and standing tall despite the unfair circumstances and trauma that has been passed onto us. Know that as well as the intergenerational trauma that's been passed on, so has the strength and resilience of our ancestors.

To my non-Aboriginal brothers and sisters – I thank you. Thank you for walking alongside us, thank you for your advocacy, for your support, for all you do to make a difference for our kids in schools and our communities. Please continue to stand with us and fight for a system that recognises our past and creates healing and nurturing for our future.

I will continue to do my part in making a difference for the change I hope to see.

> *"We need to acknowledge the past and recognise our shared histories in order to move forward with positivity and hope for a brighter future. Through an education that listens to and respects our voices, we may come to a place of healing and, perhaps, true reconciliation." (Kylie Captain)*

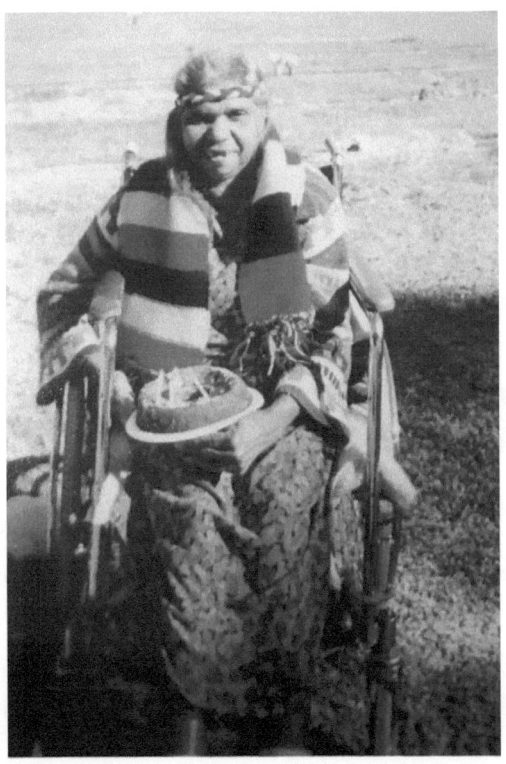

Kylie's Nan Delphine Captain. Her stories and resilience are etched in Kylie's heart and memory forever.

Kylie with Nan Delphine, and niece and nephews.
From left to right: Duane, Kylie, Jonathan,
Trent, Nan Delphine, Nathan and Kira.

Kylie with nephew Duane as a baby at her family home in Waterloo. Kylie dressed in long pants and sleeves to hide her psoriasis.

DREAM BIG & Imagine the What If

Mum Denise and Allira

Tyrell and Allira at a Survival Day event

Chapter Four

BREAKING THE CYCLE

Sadly, intergenerational trauma is evident in all cultures. At times, a vicious cycle of sadness and pain is unknowingly passed on to younger generations. Along with intergenerational trauma, the lack of hopes, dreams and aspirations of what one may think they can achieve is also passed on.

If we don't see what we aspire to be in our own families or communities, we sometimes feel that dream is out of our reach and not an option for us to consider.

I share this chapter to give hope to anyone – particularly our young people who are trying to break the cycle and make a positive change to back themselves and their ability to work towards their dreams or goals.

If you don't feel you're capable because of your upbringing, the wrong choices you've made or lack of support around you, I encourage you to take a moment to imagine the 'what if'.

What if you could be the first in your family to succeed?

What if you could prove people wrong and go on to achieve that goal?

Once you get the taste for achieving your goals, it sometimes becomes addictive, and you'll want to keep going and keep achieving more and more.

The cycle that you've found yourself in doesn't have to continue.

You can break through any barriers and find solutions to problems or hurdles that may arise along the way. You've got this!

Think about what it would do for the young people in your life if they see you achieve your dreams and goals. How good would it feel if they were to reflect on your experience and say it was because of you that they now believe they can?

To make a positive change, the first step you must take is to believe that you are worthy and allow your mind to explore all of the possibilities that await.

I often ask myself, is my story worth telling?

When the fear sets in about whether or not I should publish this book, I think about why I started. Today was a reminder.

Breaking the Cycle

I heard the devastating news that a teenage boy took his own life. I didn't know him personally; however, I know he had his whole life ahead of him. The news of his passing has deeply affected me; my heart breaks for his family and community as their world has been turned upside down.

I sat thinking to myself, *"This is not right."*

What if things didn't have to be like this?

This is a question that I often ask myself and leave with you to think about as well. Maybe through love, kindness and compassion, we can all do our part to make this world a better place. A world where all young people know that they are capable of achieving anything they set their minds to.

When we talk about breaking the cycle, I think of the fear that many of us face as it has a way of holding us back. The fear and anxiety can be paralysing.

What if you could turn that fear into resilience?

What if you could be the first to break the cycle?

The cycle that continues in many of our communities and often stops us from moving on to live rich and purposeful lives.

I know what it's like to be stuck in a cycle of sadness and fear. It's not something that I intended, however something that I felt happened quite naturally.

When I tried yarndi for the first time, it made me sick and paranoid; however, I tried it again and again, knowing that it must have some benefits because so many people I knew were smoking. I soon became aware that it made me feel good. It made me laugh and feel at ease. The pain and suffering and any sadness I was feeling would melt away.

Unfortunately, it wasn't surprising that I smoked, as many in my community did. I was stuck in the cycle, following in the footsteps of many others around me.

I remember my very first time smoking.

I stole some from my brother-in-law's stash when Mum was out one night. It was a night of laughs and fear. I remember feeling sick and scared as I heard Mum make her way through the door as she returned from the pub. I begged my sister to tell her that I was asleep if she asked for me.

Over the next year, I continued to experiment. I remember feeling terrified and paranoid; however, I continued to smoke until one day, I enjoyed it. I got to the point where I realised I was addicted. I would wake up and have cones for breakfast, lunch and dinner. I remember crying and feeling depressed if I didn't have any.

Before long, all the local drug dealers knew me, and my school attendance was low. I was only going a few times a week and often rocking in very late and sometimes stoned. I would finish school, go straight to score and smoke cones all afternoon and evening.

I got to the point where it just wasn't enough.

I became a thief and a drug addict with no hope or direction for the future. I didn't know of other strategies to bring me the same level of comfort or happiness. I didn't know how to cope with the anxiety or stress I was feeling. If only I could go back and tell my 15 year old self that it didn't have to be that way, I would tell her that there are other positive things she could do to experience joy and give her brain the good endorphins it craved. Things like speaking to someone about what she was going through, exercising, journaling, expressing gratitude, visualisation and eating healthier.

At a crucial moment in my life, a teacher did something that changed my life and opened my mind to a world of possibilities. My teacher, Ms Burgess, always went out of her way to say hello and check in to see how I was. She looked beyond my shame and low self-esteem. She made me feel smart and capable of achieving. She'd say, *"I want to see you in my Aboriginal Studies class next year. You're smart and I think you'd be amazing."*

I remember those words because of the way she made me feel.

She said it every time I saw her, until I started to think, *"What if she's right?"*

I had no intention of being in her class the following year as I didn't feel smart enough; however, in my heart, I wanted to be the first person in my family to complete the HSC.

I didn't think there was a future for me. I would get myself into unsafe situations if it meant I could get my drugs and prevent any fear or sadness from creeping back in.

Thankfully, I decided to believe her and back myself and my ability to succeed.

I looked around in my community, and there weren't many people I could look up to as role models. I wish they would've provided us kids with mentors. Some of us were shame and didn't like to speak up or go along to exciting things that might have been happening in the community. I chose to just lay low and focus on getting through each day. Thankfully I made it through those times, and now I live a happy life of freedom and choice.

I remember feeling inspired and motivated to try to make a positive change in my life.

I applied for a job at a large bank in the city. I was excited and nervous when I went to my job interview. I will never forget that experience and how the man who was interviewing me made me feel. He looked at my address and realised that I lived in Waterloo. He asked if I lived in housing commission and who I lived with. He looked me up and down like I was a piece of trash; however, he decided to continue with the recruitment process and set me up for the next hour and a half to complete the very challenging literacy and maths assessments.

As he came back in to collect my assessment paper, and without even looking at my results, he looked at me once more and said, *"I can often tell a lot about a person by their shoes and their nails and I don't think this job is for you,"* and he left.

I've never shared this story before as it still brings up so much sadness because of how he made me feel. I felt dirty and worthless, he humiliated me and left me feeling like I was never going to be good enough. I was angry with myself for going along to the interview and even thinking that I might be smart enough to work at a place like that.

This experience sat with me for a while as I went through the stages of feeling anger towards this man; however, one day I woke up, and said to myself, *"I'll show him. I'm going to make something of myself."* (I actually said far worse things about him, but for the purpose of this book I'll keep my language clean!)

I decided that I would not be a product of my environment and that I would not blame my upbringing or circumstances for how my life turned out.

I believe education is the driver of change and breaking the cycle.

We need to overcome any barriers that might be getting in the way. To the adults, if it's shoes, clothes or resources, let's get behind those kids and help them out – and to the young people, don't be shame to reach out for the help or support you need.

Let's help and encourage each other to do better and be better.

I don't know how I did it, but I managed to break through.

At 19, I became a mother, and while many may have looked at me with disappointment or thought that I wouldn't achieve or make something of myself, I took it upon myself to prove them wrong.

I was a great mum. I had so much experience caring for kids so I knew exactly what to do. It was hard at times, but I was determined to be the best possible mum I could be. I was not going to allow others' expectations of me sabotage my dreams and goals for the future.

I cared for and nurtured my son for the next two years until one day when I was in St George Bank. I decided to be brave and ask the tall, blonde woman behind the counter how to apply for a job there. I still remember her beautiful smile and how she didn't judge me for being a young mum with a two-year-old in the pram; she looked at me for who I was, a woman wanting to embark on a new career. She kindly handed over the application form and encouraged me to apply.

I spent the next six years working at St George Bank, where I was quickly promoted to a specialist position and won many awards for outstanding sales and customer service. If I hadn't have backed myself and been brave enough to give it a go, I would not have experienced this success.

We need to step outside our comfort zone and take those positive first steps if we want a better future for ourselves and our families.

What can you do to break the cycle?

Is there something repetitive or negative impacting on your ability to move forward with your dreams and goals?

Or is there someone you see potential in?

I encourage you to ask yourself those brave questions and work through any challenges that may be getting in the way.

My little unsettled spirit is still so shame; however, I continue to work hard to be the best version of myself. I don't just do this for myself, I do it to inspire and motivate others as well.

When I was at university, I created a program called *Dream Big*, an inspirational program designed to engage, inspire and motivate students about the importance of education and the power of goal setting. The program touched on topics such as self-esteem, resilience, careers, culture, leadership and attendance. A big focus was on thinking positive and the power of dreaming big.

Throughout the program, students created vision boards and engaged in journal writing as a motivational tool. The purpose of vision boards was for students to display their dreams and goals creatively. They used their journals to set goals, both short-term and long-term, and were provided with writing prompts to break down their goals into simple steps they could start doing to help them work towards their dreams and goals.

Students were also encouraged to think about their triggers and the things they needed to stop doing, and the barriers that were getting in the way.

At the end of the program, students had their vision boards and journals to take home to help keep their dreams alive.

I shared my story of growing up in Waterloo and some of the struggles I faced. The critical message was of hope and resilience along with the strategies that I learnt to pick myself up and to dream big – despite not feeling good enough or smart enough.

I felt a deep sense of purpose when delivering this program. I encouraged those kids to try to break the cycle and that inspired them to believe that their circumstances didn't have to dictate their future.

I facilitated the program in numerous schools for both Aboriginal and non-Aboriginal students. I even ran the program in Coonamble, a small country school with many Aboriginal students. The feedback from students and staff was overwhelmingly positive. This prompted me to write my book and find new and creative ways to deliver my message.

I've received so many letters and even videos from the students talking about how my story gave them hope. Some of their reflections brought me to tears.

Recently when on my way to Walgett for a funeral, I bumped into a girl in Coonamble who was in my program when she was in Year Six. She is now in Year Nine. She shared how our day together made a difference for her. She told me she was loving school and about the hopes and dreams she had for the future.

I share these stories as perhaps you may try some of the ideas I've suggested, or perhaps teachers at school may engage some positive role models to support your students.

There is something powerful about the beauty of story sharing and vulnerability. It touches people's hearts and often gives hope to others.

I have included a few reflections from students to indicate how story sharing, honesty and vulnerability impact those around us. We don't always have to put on a brave face and pretend that everything in our lives is perfect. It's also okay to admit that we've screwed up and made mistakes:

> *"I really enjoyed the talk that Kylie gave today. She went through some really tough times; however, she never gave up. She inspired me to know that I'm capable of achieving anything in life. Whenever I feel down or sad, I will always think back to this day and remember her story. She is one of the most inspirational people who I'll remember for the rest of my life. She really touched my heart. Thank you for coming to our school, Kylie. Thank you for teaching me to think positively. I dream that I too will achieve my goals, and I will be able to tell my story and reflect back on this day and talk about how you inspired me to dream big and never give up."*

> *"Hi Kylie, before you came in, I was worried about all these little things in my life. I'd just like to say thank you. I think you've changed everyone's life today. You've inspired us all to stay positive and dream big."*

"Hey Kylie, thank you so much for coming and sharing your story. You were so positive. You really did inspire me. Right now, I'm the one left behind in school. All my friends are smarter, I have bad writing and don't feel smart. I am definitely going to do better and try harder. You made me feel that I am capable of achieving anything. Thank you!"

"Hi Kylie, I like how you came into school when we needed help. You asked me what my goal was, and I told you. You spoke to me about breaking them down to short-term and long-term goals. I never thought about my dream until today. My short-term goal is to make some progress in my school work, to make new friends and finish Year 12 and maybe be the first in my family to go to uni."

I share this yarn with you to highlight the importance of story sharing and taking away the front that many of us put on, especially on social media. Everyone thinks that people live a life of luxury hidden behind the glamorous photos and extraordinary lifestyles that are reflected in their posts.

Life is about sharing, inspiring and giving hope to others.

I encourage you to reflect on this chapter and look at areas in your life or community to see where you can put a stop to negative patterns and help break the cycle.

There is always a new day and opportunity to start fresh. A chance to hit the reset button and take those first positive steps in the right direction as you never know where they'll lead.

As I reflect on my experience as a teen and the journey I've been on, I can't help but be thankful for where I ended up. I attribute my success to the power of education and the difference a teacher made. She believed in me, which opened my mind to the power of dreams and exploring the 'what if'.

All the lessons, including that interview at the bank, have allowed me to break the cycle and choose my path.

What if you took that leap of faith and had a go?

What if you stopped doing something negative and replaced it with something positive?

What if, what if, what if?

Remember, you are the captain of your ship; you choose your direction.

> *"Time waits for no one. Break the cycle and dream big for a better and brighter future for you and your mob."*
> *(Kylie Captain)*

Chapter Five

FROM FEAR TO RESILIENCE

I remember the first time hearing the word resilient and having no idea what it meant. It sounded like a big fancy word. The more I heard it, the more I was curious to know what it meant.

Resilience is the ability to bounce back from a disruption, crisis or significant life event.

As you've read in my story, I have demonstrated my resilience, time and time again. That's not to say that I don't suffer or struggle with life at times.

I am one of the most emotional people you will ever meet.

Simple things like listening to a slightly emotional speech or watching a sad scene in a movie are enough to bring me to tears instantly. I also have a high level of compassion for others. If I hear about someone going through a tough time in life, I feel for them. It sits heavy in my heart as I think of ways to help or bring happiness to their lives.

Navigating through these tough times and building your bank of strategies to help cope with an ever-changing world is essential for us all. I don't think there is anyone who will sail through life without having to demonstrate their resilience.

I acknowledge that resilience is different for everyone. Some have this incredible ability to tap into and implement their coping mechanisms, while others may struggle with identifying how to move forward.

I acknowledge that mental health is real and that many people who may be seen as not having resilience may be experiencing mental health problems.

The campaign *'It's okay not to be okay'* unpacks the stigma around mental health and opens the door for a conversation. We all know someone who struggles with mental health and at times, we all may suffer. With this in mind, we can all do our part to build a community that supports each other through life's challenges. It's important that we all have a special someone we can call on when times get tough.

When life throws us a challenge, self-doubt often sets in; however, sometimes, it's where a lot of people get stuck. Becoming stuck doesn't allow for the process of grieving and resilience to take place.

Over the years, when needed, I have spoken to counsellors and reached out to friends or family for help. I have also engaged in spiritual healing called reiki, which I've found helpful. Looking after our wellbeing and mental health is so important, and while I've shared strategies that have worked for me, you may have some of your own you can trial and share with others.

Don't ever be ashamed to reach out for help. Never suffer in silence. There is always someone or something that can help.

Once you find your resilience, there will always be fears that pop up, which often stop us from moving forward. For example, fear of judgment. Embarking on a new job, trying something different, or doing something unfamiliar to your friends, family and community can be pretty daunting. We pay so much attention to what others think and how they perceive us. At times, this stops us from moving forward with our dreams and goals. We need to take control of our lives and not allow others to choose our path. We decide where to for ourselves.

Despite finding the courage and strength to work towards my dreams and goals, I have never wanted to celebrate my success out of fear of judgement.

Unfortunately, we see it far too often, where people want to tear each other down rather than build each other up. I've decided to work through this fear and focus on my courage, knowing that I am a strong and resilient woman who simply wants to make a difference in the world.

I encourage you to find your strength, too.

Find your passion and what you love to do and work out where you want to go in life, and don't worry about what others think. As Tupac would say, *"Only God can judge me."*

Fear of failure often gets in the way of success.

Who wants to embark on a journey only to have it come back like a kick in the face if you fail. This fear often prevents us from having a go. Failure is part of life, and it helps us develop our resilience. It's what makes life interesting and challenging. When we develop our resilience, we grow both personally and professionally.

I once heard the saying, *"Either win or learn,"* and if we all use this analogy about life, we will begin to understand that life isn't always about winning; it's about learning and growing and developing our strength along the way.

There will be times when things don't work out. There will be times when you don't get that job or succeed in whatever you were trying to do; however, know that there is always a lesson to be learnt from those experiences.

Look at these times as a redirection.

We are all spiritual beings. Whenever I am faced with a decision, whether it's a job opportunity or a personal matter,

I always listen to my gut. Your gut will always give you a sign about what decision you should make. So, take the time to breathe into that feeling. See it as a silent alarm.

If things seem off or you have a nervous feeling about something, it could be a sign to back off or step away. When something feels right, and you're excited, it often means that you should move forward and give it a go.

As I write this book, those limiting beliefs have often crept back in. There is still that insecure little girl deep down inside who thinks I'm not good enough or smart enough to be an author. However, I'm choosing to push through with courage and strength, knowing that I am good enough and smart enough. I don't see myself as a writer, I'm simply someone who likes to tell a yarn.

As I reflect and share my experiences, please don't think that I have nailed it all. I've simply learnt some incredible strategies that I have trialled and implemented over the years. I still need to continue to work on myself because life is a continuous journey of self-improvement. There is always room to learn and grow.

Take the time to build up your bank of coping strategies for when times get tough.

Follow your heart and tap into your strengths and purpose in life.

> *"You are the author of your story and*
> *the writer of your dreams."*
> *(Kylie Captain)*

Chapter Six

IMAGINE THE 'WHAT IF'

People often ask how I've managed to be so driven and goal-oriented despite the challenges I've experienced. As crazy as it may sound to some, along with the power of education, I attribute my success to the law of attraction and my ancestors guiding and protecting my journey. I seek their guidance and ask for the help and support I need. I set goals and create movies in my mind of all the things I hope to achieve.

It ignites this fire in my belly, and the motivation comes from within.

The Universe sends all the people, circumstances and events my way. Don't get me wrong; I don't achieve every goal I set. Many dreams haven't turned out. However, I always see this as being steered in the right direction.

There is always a lesson to be learnt from all the dreams that don't turn out.

People often say, *"I have to see it to believe it"*; however, using the law of attraction flips that saying as if you BELIEVE you can achieve it, there is absolutely no reason why you can't.

"If you can see it in your mind, you can hold it in your hand," are the principles Mike Dooley explains in *The Secret* documentary.

The Secret can be described in three simple words, *"Thoughts become things."*

Without knowing anything about *The Secret*, a book and documentary about the law of attraction, by Australian author Rhonda Byrne, I realised I had been using it for years.

I first became aware of *The Secret* in 2008, shortly after Richard passed away. I felt like it was written for me as I had already been using many of the principles. I treat it as my bible and often turn to a random page or listen to the audiobook whenever I need guidance or inspiration.

The law of attraction has supported everything I have achieved in life.

The Secret has been used for thousands of years and by many of the world's most incredible scientists and changemakers. My idols, such as the amazing Oprah Winfrey, Gabriel Bernstein and Mike Dooley, all know and use *The Secret*, which, in essence, is simply the law of attraction.

It may sound crazy to some; however, I ask you to read this chapter with an open mind and consider the 'what if'?

Think, *"What if Kylie is on to something and what if I give it a go and what if it actually works?"*

The law of attraction is about living a positive life, visualising and seeing your thoughts and energy as magnets. Think positive thoughts and positive things come your way. Think negative, then that's what you attract.

The power of manifestation is life changing.

For example, if you're fearful about what might happen and stress about things like money, worry about being late, if you stress about bills or anticipate bad things happening in your life, those are the things that will keep turning up time and time again. The Universe responds to the kinds of thoughts we think, and many of us have a way of limiting our thinking and beliefs to what we feel we are worthy of.

As Buddha said, *"What you think you become. What you feel you attract and what you imagine you create."*

Using the law of attraction is not easy and takes consistent work. I have not mastered it all; however, I know that when I commit and put my mind to it, it never fails.

I have more than I could have ever dreamed possible, yet deep down I feel a sense of shame. I feel guilty and I wonder, why me? Why was I able to unlock the secret and apply the principles to achieve the life I desired, and others haven't?

For years, I have found it hard to celebrate my achievements out of fear of judgement. I don't want people to think I'm too good or that I've forgotten where I come from. I share now simply to inspire and give hope to others. If I can do it, I know others can too.

First, you must start to believe that anything is possible.

The law of attraction is about visualising the outcome you want.

It's about believing that what you think about most, you attract. It's about energy and the Universe giving back what you put out. If you think about an abundance of health, wealth and happiness and visualise and engage in positive experiences that support your thoughts, then that's what the Universe will deliver.

If you engage in gossip and have limiting thoughts about your ability and are stuck in the mindset of *"Why me?"* or *"Poor me?"*, then the Universe will give you more of those experiences to keep up with your own limiting beliefs and expectations of yourself.

An essential part of the law of attraction is gratitude.

The more you are grateful, the more the Universe will give you to be grateful for.

I continuously practise gratitude and give thanks for all I have.

I'm grateful for my beautiful home, for my healthy family, for my unforgettable holidays, where I've experienced different cultures and foods, something I've grown to love. My mind is so accustomed to giving thanks for every little thing. I find myself saying thank you over and over in my mind countless times a day.

As I open my eyes each morning, knowing my family is healthy and safe, I give thanks. As I turn on the tap to clean drinking water, I give thanks, and as I drive, I give thanks to my guides and ancestors for protecting my journey.

The law of attraction continues to provide me with more things to be grateful for because of the energy I put into gratitude. It might sound a bit crazy but it's what I believe and practise each and every day.

Of course, it doesn't mean that my life is perfect and I don't experience stress – trust me, I do; however, when stressful situations arise, I try to switch my energy to gratitude and give thanks for all the little things in my life. This practice usually helps me alleviate stress and shifts my energy to focus on the positives in my life.

I have many yarns I can tell you about the law of attraction and how I've used it to attract experiences, people and things into my life. My first experience was when I was 15 years old and in Year 10 at school; while this was the first experience, I didn't know the law of attraction was a thing until my mid-20s.

You may think I'm womba, but I don't care. I dare you to give it a go and look forward to you sharing your experience with me. The law of attraction allows us to use the power of the mind to turn our thoughts into reality.

The first thing we must do to use the law of attraction successfully is to become a dreamer. We need to learn to create visions and movies in our minds.

The Secret book and documentary have lots of practical examples on how to do this. We must believe that our desired outcome is already ours. We need to act as if we are receiving it, by imagining all the thoughts and feelings we would feel when we have achieved our desired outcome. I have brought myself to tears while dreaming up my goals purely by creating a movie in my mind and imagining they are already mine.

Now you think I'm womba, right? Well I guess you're womba, too, for reading this stuff! Hahaha.

Law of Attraction Yarns

My first experience with imagining the 'what if' was during my Year 10 work experience. I remember thinking to myself, *"What if I could actually get my HSC and get a deadly job like these successful blackfullas at the Department of Aboriginal Affairs?"*

Before that experience, I honestly didn't know that Aboriginal people from my community, could go on and have successful, rewarding careers in the corporate space.

As a kid, I mainly heard about athletes, activists and musicians. My dream was simple: to get a deadly job, have a family and be happy. My role now within education allows me to support educators to have these aspirational conversations with students where I encourage them to focus on their strengths and dreams. I am a fierce advocate about the importance a teacher plays in a child's life as they could be the person that makes all the difference. It did in my case.

I've worked hard to attract the things that I have achieved and experienced. I refuse to sit back and wait for life to happen.

Using the Law of Attraction

When I was about seven years old, a friend of Mum Millie came to visit. He was a whitefulla with a deadly red convertible. He took me and my sisters for a ride to his house. I don't remember much about that day apart from walking into his deadly house and lighting up with excitement as I looked towards the back of the house where I could see a pool. I remember being so excited as I was obsessed with swimming, like many kids. I headed straight towards that pool, totally mesmerised by its beauty and ran into the glass sliding door that was closed.

That image has stuck with me all of my life.

I remember how beautiful that pool was and dreamt of one day living in a home like it. I think that's where my dream started. For many years, *I remember thinking "what if one day I could own a deadly house like that?"*

From that day, throughout my life and through all the challenges, I remembered that pool and the question of 'what if' kept coming up again and again, until one day, I started to believe that I was good enough and smart enough to work towards that dream, just like anyone else.

My dream was to live a fulfilling life, making a difference in the lives of others and living in a house with a pool. It doesn't sound like much, but for me, it was huge! I went on to attract that dream of owning a house with a pool. Once I realised my potential, I thought, *"If I could achieve that dream, what else could I attract into my life?"*

I saw myself having these powers and knowledge that I should pass on to others.

The Lightbulb Moment

When I was in Year 10 and at risk of dropping out of school – as I was only going to school a few days a week and often rocking in very late – my school organised for me to complete my work experience at the Department of Aboriginal Affairs.

This was a lightbulb moment for me and one I think of often and express so much gratitude for. Without this experience, I genuinely feel that my life would have taken a very different direction. I'm so thankful that my school focused on my strengths and linked me with something that would engage me as they knew how much I loved my culture and how proud I was to be Aboriginal.

They organised for me to spend one week with the Department of Aboriginal Affairs learning all aspects of the organisation. My school took care of any barriers that prevented me from attending, such as arranging for a bus pass which allowed me to travel in and out of the city without having to pay. They also organised a $50 gift voucher, so I could buy some work clothes as I didn't have any or the money to buy them myself.

I remember this moment so clearly, and more importantly, how it made me feel.

I was so excited to try on the clothes in the shop and buy a few outfits that made me feel smart and deadly. When Mum saw me in my work gear, she cried and said I reminded her so much of Mum Millie. She told me how proud she was. I had never seen that look in her eyes before. I wanted to do well and make her proud.

I nervously took the bus from Waterloo into the city and rocked up to Wynyard with all the other morning commuters hurrying quickly through the city. I looked up at those tall buildings and all these flash people surrounding me and felt nervous.

I felt like I was a fish out of water and way out of my comfort zone.

However, I pushed on and took those brave steps and entered that building. It was like this twilight zone moment when I entered the building and saw all these deadly blackfullas dressed real flash and doing these amazing jobs.

I loved every minute of that week and made connections with all of the staff there. I had the opportunity to work in all the different sections of the department, from admin to family history research and reception. The receptionist had fallen ill on my second day, so they gave me the sole task of running the switch. I answered and transferred calls to the executive and handled that reception desk like a boss.

I felt so deadly and was on top of the world.

I was there early every day, looking smart and ready to work. I was in my element and loving life. That was the first week that I'd ever committed to anything and showed up on time every day.

Upon completing my work experience, the department asked my school if I could stay on for another week as I was doing such a great job. Gary Ella, a prominent Aboriginal figure, was leading the organisation at the time and encouraged me to stay at school and get my HSC. He told me I could work there one day and be deadly like them.

From that moment, I knew what I wanted to do. To work for an organisation that helped my people. That experience changed my life and showed me that Aboriginal people could be successful – and opened my eyes to the many careers we could embark on. It also showed me that there was a need for more of us to tap into our strengths and potential to be gamechangers for our future generations.

I knew that going on and completing my HSC would be a stepping stone for a life of freedom and choice. In 1998, I was the first person in my family to complete the HSC. It was such a proud moment for Mum as she was there at graduation to watch me receive my certificate and win awards for coming first and second in subjects as I competed with my good mate Nige. I can still see her big smile and pride in her eyes. This was the only time I remember Mum coming to school as she never felt comfortable coming in. I think it was because of her own experience.

After I graduated, I received many university offers and decided to study a Bachelor of Arts as a pathway to teaching at Sydney University. I felt that the teachers at my school made a difference for me; therefore, it was only right that I should pay it forward and follow a career in education to help other students recognise their potential and chase their dreams.

I only went to uni for a few months as I didn't have the resources and environment to study. Everything at uni required money that I didn't have. I remember them wanting $2 and $5 for course guides and the books were so expensive. I remember buying a blank raffle ticket book and walking around the uni, pretending I was selling genuine raffle tickets to make money.

It was all too hard, so I dropped out and fell back into negative habits.

I wasn't doing anything or going anywhere in life. I was smoking again with no hopes or direction for the future. That spark that I once had was gone.

The miraculous moment here and how it links to the law of attraction is a phone call that I received from a man I had met a few times over the years. He was my uncle's brother-in-law who was working for an employment agency in Newcastle.

He reached out to my family, asking for my number as he had a job opportunity he thought I might be interested in.

The job was located in Sydney. It was a Business Administration Traineeship. He just thought that by chance, either I or someone I knew might have been interested as it was an Aboriginal-identified position.

I remember this phone call like it was yesterday, and it brings me so much joy when I recall that moment.

The phone rang, and I answered it. He had to remind me a few times about who he was and I was confused as to why he was calling me. He went on to say that he worked for an employment agency, and an opportunity had come up for a traineeship. I went along with the conversation, not very interested at all. However, I politely listened and engaged in the conversation.

I was lying in bed, and all I wanted to do was go back to sleep until he mentioned that the position was at the Department of Aboriginal Affairs! I can still see myself flying up out of that bed and my whole world lighting up.

My dream of working at the Department of Aboriginal Affairs was close to becoming a reality.

I jumped up and down with excitement and told him that I was extremely interested! He said that the interviews were taking place the following morning at 9 o'clock, and he put my name down to attend.

I knew the job was going to be mine.

What a coincidence! It was so bizarre and truly meant to be. Linda Burney interviewed me, and I was offered the job on the spot. I started the very next week, and miraculously, my life was back on track.

I was an employee of the Department of Aboriginal Affairs. I was living my dream.

I know I attracted this into my life. I was sent the people, circumstances and events that allowed me to live my dream. Thank you, Universe!

Dreaming Up My House

As you've read, I am a dreamer. People asked how I do it, so this is the tell-all chapter about the way my crazy mind works. One dream, in particular, that came true was the day we bought our dream home in Sydney in 2016.

My husband and I had already bought a beautiful little red brick house with a pool and beautiful palm trees in the backyard, which I also attracted into our life. When we bought that house, everything with a pool was way out of our price range; however, I decided to make some enquiries about this particular house as it was similar to the picture I had on my vision board.

Miraculously, the advertised price was slashed which put the house into our price range, and we went on to buy that house – magic! That house was beautiful. One I dreamed up; however, it wasn't the *dream* house.

My dream house was like that flash one I visited as a kid.

This new place that I had my eye on was the one. It was like a house that celebrities and the rich and famous lived in. It was only 12 months old and had all the high-end inclusions we didn't even know existed. Walk-in robes, marble bathrooms, a chandelier, the most incredible pool, built-in outdoor kitchen … You name it, it had it.

It was mesmerising, and way out of our price range. However, I saw myself and my family living there.

Jamie laughed at me when I showed him this house and excitedly told him how I wanted to buy it. We weren't even looking to buy a house, but the Universe had other plans for us. It was number 21, which is our wedding date, and as we entered the home for inspection, I noticed the same picture and cushions that we had in the house we were living in that said, *"If you dream big enough, anything can come true."*

There was a creepy, exciting feeling the moment I laid eyes on this house and I knew it had to be ours.

Despite this dream being so far out of our reach, I had this burning desire to make it happen. I wanted to go on a journey of achieving the unachievable.

Just considering buying this house was quite an accomplishment for both Jamie and I, who had a similar upbringing. We didn't come from money and grew up with basic necessities. We were also financially supporting four children between us as Jamie also has two children from a previous relationship.

The purchase of this house really was the Universe in action. As I was searching for properties in my local area, the house popped up. It was the moment that I'll also remember forever as I instantly fell in love with it. I just felt an instant connection with it and encouraged Jamie and the kids to come and look at it with me.

It was purely out of curiosity as I knew it was way out of our price range.

The minute we walked through the door, it was like déjà vu. That moment from my childhood came back to me. I was reminded of that house where I ran into the glass door. As we walked in, I looked straight to the back where I could see this beautiful, sparkling pool that was calling my name. Everything in that house was spectacular, and all these little signs were signalling that it was the one.

The house was going to be auctioned in three weeks. It was so expensive, and never in a million years did I ever think we could afford a house like that. For the next three weeks, I was a woman on a mission, out to achieve the unachievable and buy this house. With no finance approved or even paperwork in place to get the process started, I contacted my broker.

I was an absolute crazy woman, telling him that we needed to do everything in our power to make sure this house would be ours. Jamie was in disbelief when I told him that I wanted to see if we could get a loan in place to buy the house. He has always been so supportive of my crazy dreams, so he just let me go.

It could've been a huge disaster as we miraculously arranged a bridging loan which gave us a budget to play with; however, it also meant that as a condition, we had to sell the other home we were living in within three months. After speaking with the real estate agent, I knew there was a lot of interest. I had to get the agent to convince the owner to accept my offer and take the house off the market prior to the auction as there was no way I was competing at the auction.

They would've had to drag me out of that house kicking and screaming.

For the next three weeks, I used the law of attraction.

I would sit out the front at various hours of the day and night and imagine my family living in that house. I would close my eyes and imagine putting the key in, unlocking the door and walking in with our groceries. I would visualise us taking the bins out and checking the mailbox. I would bring myself to tears of happiness about the fact that I had achieved my unachievable goal. I did this over and over again until the dream in my mind felt like it was already mine.

I wrote my name with the address of the house over and over again. I closed my eyes and saw myself jumping for joy the day that I picked up my keys. I felt the cool water rushing over my body as I took my first swim in our beautiful new pool. I imagined the candles around my beautiful, stunning bathtub in my en-suite which was covered in marble and the finest finishes anyone could imagine ...

A few days before the auction, I managed to convince the real estate agent to persuade the owner to accept my offer, which ultimately took the house off the market and secured the deal. I still can't believe I managed to pull this off! My husband cruised along on this journey in disbelief, all while smiling with pride. He often thinks I'm a bit crazy but knows that whenever I set my mind to something, there is nothing that will stop me from achieving my dream.

Everything else is a blur. We found a buyer for our house. Miraculously, someone came along and offered us the exact amount we needed within the three months and everything worked out perfectly.

I can still see the joy and the look on my kids' faces as we picked up our keys to our new home. As we rushed through the doors that summer, we headed straight for the pool.

It truly was a dream come true.

Dreaming Up My Husband

Meeting Jamie two years after Richard's death was an absolute blessing and a true example of the law of attraction responding to my thoughts and feelings. I wasn't looking for anyone. I was still so heartbroken about losing Rich. I never wanted to love again, never wanted to trust again or allow myself to feel vulnerable and open for more heartache. I still remember the pain I went through and often reflect on how things could have been if I didn't open my mind to the 'what if'.

Let me paint a picture of where things were for me and the kids at this point in our lives.

Tyrell was nine and Allira was just five years old. The past two years felt like an absolute marathon. Richard had passed suddenly, and my world was turned upside down. The next two years were pure survival. We moved five times during that time, and I managed to hold down a full-time job and travel ridiculous distances every day getting the kids to day care and school.

I worked towards achieving my goal of buying my own home as a single mother as I wanted stability in my kids' lives; I wanted to set a difficult goal, so I could look back and have something to be proud of once I achieved it. I wanted to show my kids that despite this horrible situation life had thrown our way, we were still in control of our future. We had a choice and the ability to achieve anything we set our minds to.

We loved our new home, a spacious and modern three-bedroom townhouse. The entry to the house was right down the back of the complex, which is what I loved most as I felt safe. I would drive down the driveway and straight into my double garage. It was perfect.

A few months before meeting Jamie, through my usual bedtime tears, I remember closing my eyes and imagining the 'what if'.

What if I could be in a happy relationship again?

I wondered if there was someone out there who would be right for me and the kids. It seemed like a scary thought as I knew many people who would date someone for a while, then things wouldn't turn out, and they'd be on to someone new. That's not what I wanted, as there was no way I was putting myself – or the kids through that. I hadn't really been in that situation before. Richard was my one and only long-term relationship, and I didn't have the desire or time to be dating.

I created a picture in my mind of us being happy, holidaying and being a family again. Whilst the thought did scare me, I chose to believe that perhaps it could be a possibility. I took out my journal and started to write. I really did put the Universe to the test. I started writing a list of the qualities I wanted in a partner and put it out there to the Universe.

My list included a man who would love and treat my kids with respect, no drugs, minimal drinking and a non-smoker. Someone who was hardworking, who had a big family that would love and accept both me, and my kids. Someone who was kind, generous, compassionate and trustworthy. Then I got picky, I asked for someone who was tall and cheekily added in over 6ft, handsome – and a good kisser! haha.

I thought that if it can work in other areas of my life, then I'm going to see if it'll work its magic and bring my dream man to me. I really did close my eyes and imagine this person and wondered if the Universe could deliver without all the hassle and heartache of dating and all the effort it usually takes to find the one.

This is a true story, and to my surprise, my dream man became a reality.

Around three months later, I happened to go out one night after lots of convincing from a friend. It was a friend of a friend's birthday, and they were heading into the city to an R'n'B club. Back in the day, that was what I loved to do. I had many incredible memories of being out and listening to my favourite old school jams.

I definitely wasn't looking for a man.

I did my best to avoid eye contact with any men and stayed connected to my girlfriends as much as possible. However, it was on the dance floor that I bumped into my handsome husband-to-be. It wasn't love at first sight. We had a dance and to be honest, it wasn't anything special. He was wearing a suit jacket, and I wasn't into guys who wore suits.

He was nice, handsome and tall. We exchanged numbers and spent a few hours hanging out; however, he was leaving Sydney the following day to move to Brisbane. He had just returned from overseas and was only passing through. I thought nothing of it. Over the next few months, we exchanged a few text messages from time to time, nothing serious, just the usual *"Hi, how's it going?"*

Life went on, and I don't think I had any more social outings. The kids and I were enjoying our new home, and I was working hard to pay our bills. Life was cruising along smoothly.

In those few months, Jamie had moved from Brisbane to Western Australia chasing work, then ended up back in Sydney four months later as a friend had hooked him up with a job. By coincidence, he ended up moving just ten minutes away from me. He called me to say he was back and asked if I wanted to catch up. I was so nervous and was not interested at all. It was all so scary, and I didn't know if I could do it. I had so many crazy thoughts going through my head, but my gut was telling me to say, *"Yes."*

We decided to meet for dinner at a pub and to watch a Souths game – romantic, I know. Despite the average first date, he turned out to be the man I had dreamt up. He had every quality on that list, including being over 6ft tall and an important one, having an awesome loving whanau who are everything I could have wished for – and more. Our relationship wasn't hard work, we just started hanging out, he would visit and before long, all of his stuff was at my house and he was all moved in. Oh, and the suit turned out to be a one-off – thank God!

Jamie and I have been together since the end of 2009 and have been happily married since September 2015. Together we have travelled to many beautiful places around the world and created a life beyond what either of us thought possible. We share similar upbringing and values, and both strive to be the best possible versions of ourselves.

Our motto all these years has been, *"Together we can do anything,"* and that's exactly what we've done.

Together we've achieved so much and I am forever grateful for my incredible husband. He is the kindest, caring and most humble man I have ever met. When I first met Jamie, he had $2 in his account, he was driving a gammon car and sleeping on an air mattress that continued to go flat.

Our relationship is based on respect, love and opportunity. We are blessed beyond words because we decided to give life a go and truly imagine the 'what if'.

Together we set goals and work towards achieving them. We don't only do this for ourselves, we do this for our kids and our communities. We want to lead by example and show others that it doesn't matter how or where you were brought up, whether you were rich or poor, or if you had a house or a bedroom. We want people to know the power of self-belief and to encourage our people to back themselves.

As I write this book, we are working on our latest goal of building our incredible four-storey house on our sloping block of land in the most prestigious spot in a new estate. Our land spoke to us the moment we laid eyes on it. We fell instantly in love with it and knew it had to be ours. With breathtaking views and sunsets that melt your heart, we are excited for the next chapter of our lives and seeing what lies ahead for us.

I encourage you to give using the law of attraction a go.

Start by reflecting on some of the yarns in this book or by reading or watching *The Secret*. Thinking positively can do no harm, and in fact, positive people are a joy to be around. We could all use more joy in our lives.

As I finalise this book, we are in the middle of the COVID pandemic. Australia was doing so well, and after a year and a half, it really did feel like life was getting back to normal. Things have changed with the outbreak of the highly contagious Delta variant which has made its way all over this beautiful country of ours.

People are scared and unsure of what lies ahead for us.

I don't know where things are heading or what to expect – only God knows. All I know is that I will do everything in my power to stay positive and inspire those around me to do the same. Yes, I'm scared; however, I know that fear is paralysing.

We need to support each other and lift each other up when times get tough. Life is giving us all a big assignment. We either give in to the fear and allow it to control our future, or we do everything in our power to fight back and continue to work towards our dreams and goals.

Never in a million years did any of us imagine we'd be living through something like this. Keep your thoughts positive. Give thanks for your healthy family and everything good in your life. Say it over and over. Thank you, thank you, thank you.

Dream big and imagine the 'what if' – what if life could be 'normal' again?

Close your eyes and give thanks for all the beautiful things we once took for granted.

Imagine being back there, doing the things we love.

Smile and create visions in your mind of the life you desire.

> "Thoughts become things. If you see it in your mind, you will hold it in your hand."
> (Bob Proctor)

Tyrell walking Kylie down the sandy aisle in Fiji

Tyrell giving Kylie away on her wedding day

Kylie on her wedding day

Kylie with Allira on her wedding day

Kylie and Jamie on their wedding day

DREAM BIG & Imagine the What If

Kylie and Jamie's wedding

The dream house Kylie and Jamie purchaced in 2016

The pool Kylie always dreamt of

Kylie, Jamie, Tyrell and Alllira in the Bahamas – 2018

Kylie, Jamie, Tyrell and Allira at Universal Studios LA – 2018

Kylie, Jamie, Tyrell and Allira heading to the Grand Canyon for lunch in 2018

Kylie, Tyrell, Allira and their furbaby Koda

DREAM BIG & Imagine the What If

Kylie and Jamie in Las Vegas – 2018

Chapter Seven

THE CHANGE STARTS NOW

To move towards our dreams and goals with strength and courage, we must first take ownership of where we are heading and how we are going to get there. We must acknowledge that there is no one else that can do the work for us.

Success takes courage and continuous motivation.

It's easy to become stuck and give up when we allow resentment to settle in. Blaming others for our circumstances will only cause further heartache and sadness so it's crucial we only focus on the things that we can change. We need to focus on healing from within and reconciling our past in order to dissolve any feelings of anger or guilt that block opportunities for self-love, acceptance and prosperity.

There is no denying that we are all chasing the same thing in life. Happiness.

Anyone can experience happiness. We don't need money or material things to be happy. Take a look at people around the world. Those who are from our most disadvantaged and poorest communities are sometimes the happiest. They take the time to appreciate all the little things. Despite not being born into an environment where you may have been fortunate enough to have an abundance of love, resources and happiness, it doesn't necessarily mean that you can't acquire those things.

The Universe and God will never judge you; therefore, there is always an opportunity to start fresh, to heal from within and transform your life.

Acknowledge the Pain and Sadness

Pain and sadness have a way of stopping us in our tracks. We all have a story and for many of us, our stories include parts of our journey that may include sadness. It's important that we acknowledge our pain rather than hide it. Allow it to come to the surface in order to work through it. Sometimes the easiest way to cope with pain and sadness is to mask it; however by doing this, we never quite get to experience the various stages of grief. Therefore, from time to time, the sadness continues to pop up without any warning and interrupts our lives.

You may have your own story of overcoming adversity or trauma or perhaps you've come from a broken family where you haven't had a champion in your life. Don't blame others for your circumstances, it won't bring anything good to your life. I encourage you to seek out someone who believes in you, someone who sees your potential, someone you can share your hopes and dreams with.

Pray about it and keep an eye out for the signs; there is someone out there for everyone.

Forgive What Has Caused You Pain

Holding on to pain and anger is no good for us. The Bible talks about forgiveness and how important it is in life. I look at forgiveness as a way of self-healing. Forgiveness is not to benefit those who have caused the pain or sadness in our life; it is purely for our own peace and wellbeing.

Holding on to anger and sadness blocks us from moving forward with positivity.

Close your eyes and imagine the person or situation that has caused sadness in your life. Take a big deep breath in and hold it, then exhale. Repeat this a few times. Place your left hand above your navel which is where your intuition sits, and now place your right hand above your heart.

Say to yourself, *"I forgive you,"* repeat it over and over, *"I forgive you, I forgive you, I forgive you."*

Try including a positive affirmation such as, *"I forgive those who have caused me pain. I choose to forgive in order to receive love and positivity. I am strong and resilient and I choose to live life on my terms, not anybody else's."*

Whilst it's easy to carry anger and bitterness for those who have hurt us, for our own peace and joy, we need to let go.

Find Your Courage

I've been listening to a meditation around courage and find it's helped me to stay focused on my purpose and is a nice reminder about why I started this journey of writing. The process of writing has been one of healing and I thank you for allowing me to share my story with you.

Nelson Mandela once said, *"It always seems impossible until it's done."*

Every new journey is hard however; you will never know if you will succeed unless you try.

I encourage you to take that leap of faith and believe in yourself.

Look at yourself in the mirror and say some positive affirmations to help ignite that fire within your belly and then embark on whatever it is you wish to achieve.

Say to yourself, *"I am good enough and I am smart enough. I'm healthy and full of love and life. I forgive myself for not being perfect, as no one is. I trust the journey of life and know that everything that I have experienced has led me to where I am today."*

Write Yourself a Script for Healing

We're good at giving advice to others; however often when it's ourselves who need help, we don't give it our full attention. Imagine what you're experiencing or wanting to embark on is not yours but that of a friend.

What advice would you give them?

What would you tell them to start doing and what to stop doing?

Write it down like a script from a doctor. Believe that you matter, just as much or more than anyone else in your life.

Commit to the Process of Healing and Growing

Despite the many challenges that have been thrown my way, one thing that has always kept me strong is my ability to put myself in the shoes of others.

Despite the grief and sadness that I've experienced, I always thought about those less fortunate than I.

I find strength in reflecting on all the things that I'm grateful for. Little things, such as running water and a roof over my head and the comfort and safety of my family surrounding me.

I encourage you to think about these things that we often take for granted.

Know that you are incredible, loving and kind. You have been directed to receive this book for a reason. Circumstances, people and events always come our way for a reason. Know that there is no coincidence that you are reading this book.

Ask yourself, *"What is the lesson that this story is trying to teach me?"*

In the words of Dr Seuss, remember:

> *"You have brains in your head.*
> *You have feet in your shoes.*
> *You can steer yourself any direction you choose.*
> *You're on your own.*
> *And you know what you know.*
> *And YOU are the one who'll decide where you go…*
> *Oh, the places you'll go!"*

Think about all the things that you would love to do if there was absolutely no chance of failing.

Help Someone Along the Way

How good does it feel when we are in a position to help someone?

Research shows that when learning new information, by teaching someone else, it actually helps us absorb the information and learn. Find yourself a buddy or someone who you feel could use some positivity in their life. Share some of the things you have learnt and have started to implement in your life. Don't be embarrassed about embarking on a journey of positivity. Others will admire your strength and courage and you might also inspire them to make a positive change in their life.

Don't feel you have to hold on to all this new knowledge to yourself. Know that there's enough good in the world to go around.

The Change Starts Now

There is no better time than now. Commit to the change you want to see in your life. Remember that time waits for no one. It is never too late to start something new. You may want to utilise my Dream Big Journal as a treasured item to help get your dreams and goals out of your head and onto paper – that is the first step. As you progress, it's amazing to watch them manifest into reality.

Remember, the only person who can stop you is you.

It's important to reflect on those limiting beliefs and continue the positive self-talk to help you stay focused. Know that you are worthy of this change. You have attracted it into your life.

Learn to Love Yourself

Know that you are unique and beautiful in your own way. How boring would this world be if we were all the same? Love every part of your being.

Love yourself into healing.

Have you ever looked back at a photo and thought to yourself, *"Gee, I look good in this pic"*; however, at the time, you don't remember feeling good?

Those limiting beliefs and lack of self-love prevent us from seizing the moment and engaging in that feeling of love. In order to fully love others, we also need to learn to love ourselves.

Look in the mirror and acknowledge and give love to every part of your body. The more you love yourself, the more the Universe will send you things to be grateful for and more things to love about yourself.

Remember like attracts like and love attracts love.

It's never too late to decide who and what you want to be.

> *"The biggest adventure you can take is to live the life of your dreams. Having the courage to stand up and pursue your dreams will give you life's greatest reward and life's greatest adventure."*
> *(Oprah Winfrey)*

Chapter Eight

THE TEACHER IN ALL OF US

We all have a role to play in teaching, inspiring and motivating our young people to believe in themselves and chase their dreams. Everyone is responsible for ensuring our kids reach their full potential in all aspects of life and learning.

We are all teachers, every single one of us.

Aboriginal Australia is the longest-living surviving culture because of how well we cared for the land and each other. The passing of knowledge from generation to generation has been an integral part of keeping our culture alive for tens of thousands of years. Teaching the younger generations about essential things such as kinship, totems and land management is a necessary part of life.

We all have a responsibility to learn and, importantly, to impart our knowledge to others. Uncle Bob Morgan, a respected educator and researcher, recently explained that stories are critical and integral to Aboriginal pedagogy. Therefore, they should be incorporated into various curricula to truly and effectively engage students and improve learning outcomes. His words resonated deeply as I understand the importance of story sharing and the tremendous impact they have in engaging students in learning.

Stories are the foundation of all knowledge, both in and out of the classroom.

As a proud Aboriginal woman and educator, I've taken the role of a teacher very seriously. I love kids and feel so happy when I see my beautiful nieces and nephews. I am a favourite aunt to many, and I believe it's more than the fact that I have a deadly pool to spend their summers in; I think it's because of how I make them feel.

I acknowledge their presence and get excited when they enter the room. I love hearing about what they've been doing and all they've been learning. My joy always shows in my body language and my voice about how genuinely interested I am in what's happening in their lives.

As parents and carers, aunties and uncles, we all have a responsibility to teach. I have taken my natural ability to teach and obtained a formal qualification as a trained primary school teacher; however, I acknowledge the important role families and communities play in educating our young people. They are their first teachers.

It's essential to be present in our young people's lives.

Think back to your childhood. What are the things that stand out in your memory? I'm sure you'll agree that it's the experiences where you felt excited or acknowledged. I remember we had a calendar on the wall at home when I was about 10. There was a quote on this particular page which I had memorised. I remember my Uncle Stuart coming to visit and I was excited to read it to him. I pretended I was reading the words; however, I had only memorised the phrase. I remember him saying to my Mum, *"Eya, she deadly this one."*

I remember grinning from ear to ear as I felt so smart and deadly.

We all are busy and live in a fast-paced and demanding world where technology is at our fingertips; therefore, I feel it's critical that we take the time to get back to the basics of how our kids learn.

Poet and civil rights activist Maya Angelou said, *"People will forget what you said, people will forget what you did, but people will never forget how you made them feel."*

This is an essential aspect of teaching. I try my best to ensure I live my life, personally and professionally, with this quote embedded into my everyday practice.

Our words and actions are powerful, and it is crucial that we, as teachers, leave a lasting impact on those around us.

Be Present in Your Kids' Lives

Whilst parenting is one of the most incredible blessings anyone could experience, I acknowledge that it is not easy, particularly with social media challenges these days. The bullying and negativity reported around social media usage is astonishing.

Without being brave enough to say mean things face to face, social media provides a platform to take bullying to a whole new level. Depression and low self-esteem is often reported in many of our youth today. We must let our kids know that we are there for them and will never give up on them. I can't stress the importance of lighting up when our kids walk through the door. That human connection and feeling can't be done through text messaging – we need to show and have them feel how much we love and care for them.

As a mother, my goal was and still is to raise good humans. Whenever I would receive their report cards, I would never worry about what grade they would receive; I would always skip straight to the comments to read the part where they talked about the type of people they were. I wanted to know if they had tried their best and were respectful, kind and caring. Those are the things that I would express most gratitude for.

Being a mother is my most treasured attribute.

I love my kids more than anything in this world and nothing makes me prouder than to see them thriving and doing well in life.

I encourage you to take the time to be present with your young people. Get excited when they walk through the door and show interest in what's going on in their lives. I am sometimes guilty of not being present, especially with social media and the demands of work. I have to always gently remind myself to be present and to sit and yarn.

As a parent, I feel it's important to always talk to your kids from a very young age. Those early years are fundamental for brain development and building trusting relationships. For example, talk to them about what you're doing in the kitchen and the things you're buying in the grocery store. This helps with their learning and preparation for school.

Prior to my career in education, I worked in child protection and early intervention services, where I would support some of our most vulnerable families to access support to help them be the best possible parents. The best advice I could give my clients was to talk to their kids, smile at them, hug them, and be mindful of their words and actions.

In Aboriginal culture, stories and lessons have been passed down from generation to generation orally and through art, song and dance. I feel that story sharing is such a powerful form of communication and is imperative for good teaching practice. There is something so powerful about the beauty of telling and listening to stories. I love to yarn and feel that beautiful human connection that storytelling brings.

I encourage you to tell your kids stories of your upbringing and your past. Share with them all the wonderful things you remember as a child, the stories that were passed down from your parents and grandparents.

We need to keep our stories alive to pass down our legacy and knowledge to future generations.

Good Pedagogy Is Key

When I first started studying education, I had no idea what the word pedagogy meant. It sounded like a very fancy word that was not part of my vocabulary. However, I soon learnt that pedagogy meant the art of teaching; the way and how you teach.

Good pedagogy is essential for successful teachers. If you know how to engage your learners and teach in a fun and inclusive way, you're a pretty deadly teacher.

When I think back to my journey as a classroom teacher, it is something that I naturally excelled at. My first class was Year One/Two (six and seven year olds), which I was thrilled about. There is something super cute about those little ones who are just losing their baby teeth. They look up to you like you are the most important person in the world.

Every day I went to school, I felt like a celebrity; even on those days where I felt like crap. The moment I saw my kids, all my worries would melt away.

The Teacher in All of Us

I quickly excelled as a classroom teacher, often sharing new teaching methods with colleagues who had been in the profession for years. I incorporated certain things into my pedagogy that every teacher should include, things like checking in. It's essential to check in with kids in the morning and just like you would as a parent or carer, get excited when they walk in the room. For some of our students, particularly those who may not get this from home, a teacher may be the first person who has smiled at and greeted the child that day.

As humans, we all crave to be valued and acknowledged.

If you want to improve educational outcomes, you have to improve relationships. The moment you lay eyes on a child, get excited! Check in with them and ask them how they are. Show them you care and how much you believe in them. Get excited about the day ahead and all of the learning that will take place.

Every morning before we started the day, my class would check in. I had a beautiful big yarning circle mat in my classroom. We would all sit in a circle and make sure everyone was okay. Sometimes we would go around the circle and say one word or a sentence about something we are grateful for or something we were hoping to learn that day. Sometimes we will just have a thumbs up, thumbs down, or in between.

Doing this allowed me to see who was feeling great, and importantly, it allowed me to see those kids who potentially may not have had a good morning or were feeling a bit off.

As a class, we all took responsibility to make sure that we looked after each other. I created an environment where everyone belonged and where everyone cared about the wellbeing of each other first and foremost.

I had some challenging students in my class that year; however, something I am most proud of as a teacher was the ability to build relationships with each and every one of my students, parents and carers. They knew that I was there because I cared and wanted to make a difference, which led me to achieve great results as a teacher.

I share these yarns because I want to inspire teachers to never underestimate the importance of relationships. Without positive relationships, the goal of achieving improved outcomes and engagement at school is going to be extremely challenging.

The Importance of Story Sharing

Disconnected facts mean nothing to students; therefore, as a classroom teacher, I would always start every lesson with a yarn and tell my students a story about how that particular lesson would benefit them in the future. I would share a story about a real-life situation, so students would engage and know how to apply that piece of learning to a real-life experience. For example, if I were teaching a lesson about money, I would share an exciting story about going grocery shopping or putting petrol in my car and needing to make sure I had enough money to buy my kids Maccas as a treat.

When teaching literacy, I would talk about the need to write a job application in the future and how that job could give them all the money and resources they needed to help their families or buy all of their favourite things. As I told the stories, I could see the students engage and light up because they connected the learning to a real-life scenario.

As a mother, there have been so many times that my kids have come home complaining about not knowing when they would ever use a particular lesson in real life. Armed with this information, I took everything I knew about engaging kids into the classroom as a teacher.

As educators, we must have fun with the creative process. We need to develop fun and engaging ways to ensure that our lessons will be absorbed. A simple engagement strategy that often helps is to allow students to take part in the planning. This ensures they feel valued and smart, and a part of the entire learning process.

Focus on the Strengths

Never underestimate the power of positive feedback. When giving feedback to students, always start with the positives and don't ever shame or scrutinise students. Once their confidence has been shattered, you may never get it back.

Our most challenging students need so much love, care and compassion.

Yes, they are hard work, and yes, they may drive you nuts, but you entered into the world of teaching knowing that there would be many different personalities, styles of learning and backgrounds in your class.

Rita Pierson said, *"Kids don't learn from people they don't like."*

It's up to us as educators to work on developing trusting relationships with students and their families. Teaching is an important job. Think creatively about ways to bring out the best in students. Find ways to allow them to shine.

Once you've developed trusting relationships that are strength-based, those hard conversations won't be so difficult.

Positive relationships with students and families improve student outcomes.

Never stop believing in a child.

Allow Students to See Themselves in the Curriculum

There is nothing more that students love than to discuss their cultural background and the things they are experts in. It allows them to feel included and valued.

Throughout the year, there are many opportunities where Aboriginal content can be easily weaved throughout the curriculum.

Start with the Aboriginal calendar and look at all the dates and significant events throughout the year. Use these as teaching points to engage your Aboriginal students and teach all students about the rich and beautiful culture that is there for everyone to engage with.

There are so many incredible resources available on the internet; however, it's important to never underestimate the value that local families and communities can offer. Remembering that relationships don't happen overnight, and you as the educator may need to build those relationships before families and communities develop that trust and add value to your teaching.

When teaching, always refer to things in the local community that students can relate to. Think about all the things they can see, feel and touch. Of course, in this day and age, we have an abundance of resources readily available on the Internet; however, never underestimate that human experience of seeing and touching.

Good teaching allows students to demonstrate their knowledge and experience in many different ways.

Using various assessment practices will enable students to tell you what they have learnt verbally. This can be used as a powerful assessment of learning. Some students may not cope well with tests; however, they will happily tell you a yarn about what they've learnt. Some students may prefer to show you. Every student learns differently; therefore, they should have the opportunity to demonstrate new learning in various ways.

We are all teachers and lifelong learners, continuously reflecting and finding creative ways to improve our practice.

As teachers, parents and carers, we all want the same thing, for our kids to grow into incredible humans and be the best possible version of themselves. We need them to know that they are smart and deadly and capable of achieving anything they set their minds to.

Never stop believing in our kids.

> *"We all have a role to play in teaching, inspiring and motivating our young people to believe in themselves and chase their dreams."*
> *(Kylie Captain)*

Chapter Nine

EVERYONE DESERVES A CHAMPION

Luckily for me, I had a champion at school. I had a few actually and if it wasn't for these incredible educators who looked past my poor attendance and lack of resources to be ready to learn, I don't know where I'd be today.

There's one teacher that comes to mind from my time at Redfern Public School. Her name was Ms Bosler. She had beautiful, blonde hair and a deadly red car. I loved going to school as I knew that she would light up with excitement whenever she saw me. Often, I went to school for this interaction, mainly because of the way she made me feel.

I was also lucky enough to have an amazing principal and some deadly teachers in high school who made me feel like I could be someone. They took the time to build a relationship with me. They asked me questions about what I was interested in and showed interest in my responses. How they treated me made a difference. They treated all of us kids as humans and individuals. They cared about us and valued what we had to say.

There was one teacher, in particular, at Cleveland Street High School (Clevo), who stands out as the one who made all the difference. Ms Burgess who was not only a champion then, she still is now.

Years after I finished school, I emailed her to tell her I was thinking about enrolling in a teaching degree at university. I knew it would be a mission as I wanted to hold down my full-time job, study a full-time uni course and raise my young kids. I asked her what she thought and if she felt it was achievable. She simply replied saying, *"You're smart, you can do it."*

Her belief in me gave me all the confidence I needed.

I'm now fortunate enough to work alongside her as the Vice President of the Aboriginal Studies Association. She is now known as Associate Professor Cathie Burgess, a wonderful woman who has done so much for Aboriginal Education throughout her career. She is an incredible example of a true champion, and my goal is to inspire more champions both in and out of the classroom.

I did exceptionally well at university and was fortunate enough to be placed on the Dean's Merit List year after year for my outstanding academic achievement, where my average grade was high distinction and distinction. Mum always said I had 'the brains', and I guess I just needed the opportunity and the self-belief to put myself to the test.

We all need someone to see the potential in us that we don't often see ourselves.

There are certain things that teachers can do to make a difference for students. High expectations are paramount as if the teacher doesn't believe that the student can learn, then it is highly unlikely they will.

Everybody has a brain and the ability to learn.

Having a growth mindset where we back ourselves and our ability enhances the learning process. If you are a teacher, I encourage you to get to know your students. Have aspirational yarns with them, find out what they like and how they best learn. Students know when you mean something and can see right through you when you fake it.

Teaching isn't just about teaching the content; it's about inspiring and changing lives. If students see you as genuine and caring, they will learn to trust you and take risks in their learning. As an educator, this is something that I have focused on throughout my career.

Educators need to focus on students' strengths and build upon them. Don't focus on the fact they are late; focus on the fact that they are there. Have high expectations through positive relationships. I believe teachers can bring out unlimited potential in learners.

Using these practical strategies won't dramatically improve outcomes overnight.

Change takes time, as do positive relationships to form.

I have so much respect for the incredible teachers out there. They are teachers, counsellors, event coordinators, artists, scientists, mathematicians and family support workers.

As much as students need champions, so do we as adults. It's essential to give thanks to the extraordinary mentors in our lives. I owe so much of my success to the wonderful mentors and champions in my life.

There have been many champions throughout my career.

I have been lucky enough to work with incredible leaders who saw the best in me in every workplace. A few, in particular, are my beautiful friends and colleagues, Nat and Sherrie. Both were my supervisors who saw my potential and have supported my leadership journey. As they have grown as leaders, they have never forgotten to leave the door open to allow others to follow in their footsteps.

Sherrie is the most organised person I know, and Nat has inspired me with her gift of storytelling and how to bring people along on the journey through positive relationships, a strength I admire. With her leadership and support, I have stepped into her previous role as the Glenfield Aboriginal Education Team Leader, a team and work-family I love and give thanks for every day.

After I finished my university degree, I nervously waited for the call to find out which school I was appointed to. It was a nervous time as I was going from a successful career to taking a step back both professionally and in pay to be the new kid on the block as a beginning teacher. I knew that to get ahead in my career and fulfil my lifelong dream of changing students' lives, I had to take that step. I had aspirations to become a leader in Aboriginal Education and to get there, I needed a principal who would support me and allow me to flourish.

My prayers were answered as I was aligned to a school with the most incredible principal, Mike Newcombe, who is a passionate advocate for Aboriginal Education and was an absolute champion for me. He and his executive staff, Kylie and Michelle, allowed me to flourish and focus on my strengths. I formed trusting relationships with the students, parents and staff and thrived as a beginning teacher as I brought years of knowledge and experience from my previous roles. I was a natural, and I was living my dream as a teacher and making a difference.

I recall our director, Maria, visiting my classroom. She left me feeling valued and appreciated as she gave me the most incredible compliment as she said *"I would love to be a student in your class"* – I knew I was making a difference. My dream had come true.

Without the support of these incredible leaders and the way they believed in me, I don't know if I'd be where I am today.

I am forever grateful for the guidance and support from the champions in my life. The people in my corner who are there to uplift and motivate me. Those who clap the loudest when I succeed and those who have my back no matter what.

I encourage you to find your circle of people.

Think about those who believe in you.

Think about the way they make you feel.

Do they uplift and inspire you? If not, keep searching.

Ask for the signs, follow your gut and trust that the Universe will always have your back.

We all need champions and people who believe in us to remind us of our dreams and goals and tell us we're doing a good job.

Who can you be a champion for?

I'm a big believer in karma – what you give is what you get. I encourage you to reflect on where you are in life and who has been a champion for you. Reach out and thank them for what they've done.

Find someone to champion.

Let them know you see their strengths.

Tell them what you admire about them.

We can all be champions and do our part to make the world a better place.

> *"Every child deserves a champion, an adult who will never give up on them, who understands the power of connection, and insists that they become the best that they can possibly be."*
> *(Rita Pierson)*

Kylie with Associate Professor Cathie Burgess, the teacher who was a champion for her

Kylie proudly leaving her handprint at Western Sydney University – Badanami Centre for Indigenous Education after graduating with a Bachelor of Education (Primary) – Aboriginal and Torres Strait Islander Education

Everyone Deserves a Champion

Kylie on her university graduation day

Kylie, Jamie, Tyrell and Allira at
Kylie's university graduation

Chapter Ten

DEADLY SECRETS TO SUCCESS

Success is about doing our absolute best in life and making the most of opportunities despite what life throws at us. Over the years, I have always strived to be the best version of myself, to show up time after time with positivity and perseverance.

To be successful, we first need to identify what success means to us. It could be successfully quitting smoking, completing a course or mending a broken relationship.

There is no right or wrong when it comes to success, and success for each and every one of us is different. I've always been someone who's been career-driven and someone who has continuously tried to push boundaries to see what I was capable of.

My goal and mantra have always been to show up and do my best. I've always said that if others are able to learn then so can I. This new version of myself is very different to the old me where I wanted to cruise quietly through life without standing out as I didn't feel I was good enough for success.

Here, I'm going to share practical strategies that anyone can use to start working towards their dreams and goals. The things I've trialled and implemented and have helped me set goals, stay focused and committed throughout my dreaming process.

I encourage you to select three and start doing them daily.

I always say that good things come in three.

It's said that it also takes three weeks to form a new habit so when you start, try your best to stick with it for three weeks to see lasting change.

Know that any day is a good time to start. You don't have to wait until Monday or the start of a new month or new year. Know that you can start NOW!

Since I was a little girl, I've always believed in God. I always remember having faith that there was something bigger than me, like a higher power or energy source. I believe I have spirit guides, God and my ancestors, protecting and watching over me.

The first thing that I do when I want to set a new goal is I pray about it.

I encourage you to do so, as well. Even if you don't believe in God, pray to your ancestors, pray to your loved ones who have passed or even just verbalise your intentions to yourself.

The first step in using the law of attraction is to ask.

Verbalise it and put it out there to the Universe.

Every morning, I wake up and go through my morning routine. I do things like meditate, journal, exercise and express gratitude.

I find it allows me to set my intention for the day and focus on achieving it. It also gives me time to get energised, reflect and give thanks for everything in my life.

From the minute I wake up, the first thing that I do in my mind is to say thank you.

Thank you to God.

Thank you to the Universe.

Thank you to my old people.

Thank you to my angels for their endless love and protection.

Over the years, I've read countless personal development books and listened to many podcasts and audiobooks about showing up and being the best version of myself. I'm going to attempt to share some the things that have helped me in the hope they may do the same for you.

As mentioned, I encourage you to choose three things – just three and try your best to do them at least three times a week. It doesn't have to be very long; you could choose to spend five to ten minutes doing each of these things, so just 30 minutes out of your day.

That doesn't sound like much, does it?

Maybe find yourself an accountability partner to help you stick to it.

Think about how much time we spend mindlessly scrolling through social media each day. You can do it!

Our minds are good at playing tricks on us. There will always be negative thoughts that creep in. I label them as blockers. They show up unannounced and try to convince you to make up excuses for why you can't commit to your plan.

For example, they may cause you to think that there isn't enough time in the day, or that you can't do it because you didn't sleep well or because it's too cold, or you feel sick, etc. You need to get moving before you start to believe and give in to these blockers.

Know that dreaming big and visualising what you want will NOT work without taking ACTION.

You need to get up, show up and do something. Start by setting your alarm clock half an hour earlier. I find that waking up at 5:00 a.m. or 5:30 a.m. are great times to wake as it gives me plenty of time to work through my morning routine and plan my day. I don't do it all the time; however, when I do, I feel amazing!

When the blockers creep in and encourage me to sleep in until 7:00 a.m. or 8:00 a.m., I often wake up feeling tired.

I remember when my son was participating in the Wimp to Warrior mixed martial arts program. He was the youngest participant at just 17 and in his last year of school. It was a six-month challenge where he would train for an hour and a half at 5:00 a.m. every morning before school. When he asked if he could participate, I was so scared.

I thought he was mad for wanting to do such a thing.

However, I knew he was a good kid, and I wanted to support his wellbeing during his HSC. His goal was to go the entire six months without missing a day. He set goals and wrote as if he had already achieved them. He wrote something along the lines of, *"I'm so happy that I've just completed this program. I went every single day for six months, with zero days off."*

He set his intention and put it out there to the Universe.

His dedication was admirable. He went the entire time without missing a day. Their motto was 'while they were sleeping' – meaning while everyone else was sleeping, they were up, training and smashing out their dreams and goals.

How can you move towards your dreams and goals?

Surround yourself with people you admire.

If you like a particular person for their strengths or courage or how they respectfully interact with others, rub shoulders with them and find opportunities to interact with and learn from them.

Think about how certain people make you feel. Do they make you feel happy, or do they cause you to feel anxious, worried or stressed?

I believe we always need to look after ourselves before we can look after anyone else. It's taken me a long time to learn to protect myself from unwanted negative energy. What I've learnt over the years is that unless my wellbeing is taken care of, I'm no good to anyone else.

We must always look after ourselves first.

Goal Setting and Journaling

Buy yourself a journal.

It doesn't have to be anything fancy, you can use my Dream Big Journal or a $2 notebook from Kmart or Coles.

Start by writing your thoughts about the goals you're hoping to achieve. Some prompts could include short-term and long-term goals and what you're going to start doing to achieve them. What you're going to stop doing is also very important. The people you need to spend more time with and the ones you need to keep your distance from. Think about what your ultimate goal would be if there were absolutely no way of failing.

Use this as a guide or come up with your own headings and start the process of goal setting. You may even want to share your goal with an accountability buddy.

Write down your thoughts as if you've already achieved your goals. For example, I'm so happy and thankful as it's been six months, and I have not had a single cigarette, or for the past two years, I've been saving and can now afford my new car or have a deposit for my new home. Get excited and describe all your feelings, as if you have already achieved your goals.

Having our goals written down is a powerful thing that is difficult to understand until you start the process.

Just putting pen to paper is an extremely therapeutic exercise to support our wellbeing. You can write about how you're feeling, something that's frustrating you, or things you're grateful for.

Give it a go and watch your life transform.

Vision Boards

After watching *The Secret* in 2008, I thought it was silly to create vision boards as part of the visualisation process.

However, once I used them a few times, I realised how powerful they are. I'd put up pictures of a deadly house, positive quotes or new holiday destinations.

Vision boards truly are incredible.

They help keep our dreams alive, reminding us why we started and are a powerful form of defence when those blockers creep in. For example, when I wanted a house with a pool and a puppy, I put pictures up reminding me of my goals. I had a photo of a pool with palm trees surrounding it; however, buying a house with a pool was way out of our price range. I believe having this image on my vision board helped bring my dream to fruition.

It's also a fun exercise you can do with your family. Get the kids involved and start the goal setting process from a young age. All you need is some magazines or pictures and quotes from the internet, a frame or corkboard, scissors, stickers and pencils. Some of the students I worked with in the Dream Big program loved making vision boards because it's such a therapeutic exercise. It made them feel good and was a nice visual to help keep their dreams alive once the program had ended.

The Power of Visualisation

Visualisation and manifesting are a crucial part of the dreaming process.

It's as simple as creating a movie in your mind about what it is that you want to achieve. You just need to close your eyes and visualise the end result of what you're hoping to achieve. Don't think about all the things that you need to do to get there. You've already done that.

Manifesting is about celebrating success.

Don't think about the process and all the hurdles you need to get through along the way, fast-forward till the end. Visualise the phone call when you've been told that you were successful. See yourself jumping up and down with joy and excitement. You can also visualise telling someone the great news. Feel all the feelings as if you've already achieved it. Remember to always say thank you, thank you, thank you!

When things don't work out there is always a lesson to be learnt from the process or the Universe steering you in another direction.

Everything happens for a reason.

The Power of Prayer and Asking for Guidance

I am not an overly religious person. I don't go to church; however, I do believe in God.

Usually, people only ask for help when something is going terribly wrong in their lives or they're experiencing turbulence on a plane; however, part of my recipe for success is to seek guidance and ask for the help and support you need in your everyday life. Whatever it is that you need, just ask and show gratitude for receiving.

One of my favourite authors and spiritual guides, Gabrielle Bernstein, shared this prayer from *A Course in Miracles* that I love:

"Where would you have me go? What would you have me do? What would you have me say? And to whom?"

Gabby says to stop praying for what we think we need but pray for what is of the highest good for all. Take your hands off the wheel and let the Universe guide you to where you're meant to be.

Keep an eye out for the people, circumstances and events to guide you on a path to living your purpose.

Positive Affirmations

We all need positivity in our lives.

The late Louise Hay has been an incredible influence in my life. She is the queen of positive self-talk. Because of my background of not feeling good enough or smart enough to be successful, I have had to work extremely hard to back myself and often use positive affirmations to fight the blockers in my head. I still use this powerful tool when that insecure little girl creeps back in who feels she isn't smart or good enough to be embarking on some of my big adventures. Louise said to look in the mirror and tell yourself things like, *"I'm good enough, I'm smart enough and people like me."*

She has an abundance of affirmations; however, this is one that most resonated with me. You may like to incorporate this practice into your routine. It's a simple process that can be used anywhere. Don't point the finger or blame others if you don't have that special someone to believe in you.

Instead, back yourself and set out on a journey of living your best life.

Select Your Circle

Have an accountability group or someone who is aware of your goals and can check in on you from time to time or join a positive Facebook group where you'll be surrounded by a community of people to uplift and inspire you.

Surround yourself with people who make you feel good and bring out the best in you. Whenever I'm feeling down or need some uplifting, I always call my deadly sista, Bronwyn. She and I have been so close since we were young, and she's the only person who can literally make me feel like I'm going to wet myself with laughter. We've been laughing about the same things for over 25 years. We understand each other on a deeper level than we sometimes know ourselves. I'm grateful to have had my sista by my side all of these years. From partying hard to losing teeth but most importantly, for all the memories we've shared. The memories that will last a lifetime.

I give thanks each and every day for my beautiful sista and all the other positive people in my life who continue to uplift and inspire me.

Choose your circle wisely. Try your best to replace the drainers with those who bring out the best in you.

The Five Second Rule

Mel Robbins, author of the book, *The Five Second Rule*, talks about getting up within the first five seconds of your alarm. We've all set our alarms in hope to wake up early and go to the gym (this is often a struggle for me). She talks about psychology and how our minds operate. Mel states that if we don't start moving within five seconds of our alarm going off, all those negative thoughts and blockers start creeping in and sabotage our good intentions.

Get up and show up for all those good intentions you've set for yourself.

The Power of Exercise

Spending just ten minutes in the morning engaging in some form of exercise can dramatically improve your life.

I have never been a consistent exerciser, however, when I do engage in regular exercise, especially in the morning, I find I have a whole new level of positivity.

Find a routine that you can implement first thing in the morning. Perhaps join a gym or commit to a brisk walk or even just dropping down and doing sit-ups, push-ups and stretches is enough to get the blood and positive thoughts flowing. I often feel I have so much more energy after I have exercised compared to those times when I let the blockers tell me I should prioritise sleep over getting up and starting my day right.

Meditation

Recently, I've been listening to podcasts on the Chopra app, created by Oprah Winfrey and Deepak Chopra. I find it's making a difference in my focus and tapping into my courage, especially during this writing process. I have attempted to engage in meditation over the years; however, I always find it hard to stay focused. My mind is always wandering off thinking about something else rather than the task at hand, which is to remain present.

One thing I try to do is say the word 'aware' when I feel my mind wander.

Sometimes fear sets in, and we may think fearful thoughts about the past or things we're scared of happening in the future. Know that the past and the future does not matter at that point in time, particularly when those fearful thoughts creep in. When done correctly, meditation can bring a whole new level of clarity and purpose to your life.

Give it a go and see what it does for you.

I encourage you to pick three of the suggestions above or create some of your own and start by setting up your regular morning routine.

Spend at least ten minutes on each and watch your life improve dramatically.

> *"We are magnificent beings, capable of achieving anything we set our hearts and minds to. Once you convince your mind that you are capable, there is no stopping you."*
> *(Kylie Captain)*

Chapter Eleven

WHETHER YOU THINK YOU CAN, OR YOU CAN'T, YOU'RE RIGHT

There are endless possibilities when we think about the law of attraction and how we can implement it into our everyday lives. There's a whole lot of evidence and science behind it and how it's related to quantum physics. It is often described as a magnificent force of energy that attracts the people, circumstances and events that our thoughts have manifested. Many people call these things coincidences; however, as crazy as I may sound, I believe that everything in our lives is because of our thoughts and the things that we have attracted.

Many of the strategies shared in this chapter have been inspired by Rhonda Byrne, author of *The Secret*. Here, I share practical examples of how I have taken some of the suggestions and applied them to my everyday life.

I shared my experiences using *The Secret* and how I manage to dream up many things in my life. I believe in it and I live by it. I'll now share some simple things that you may try to implement in your life. I dare you to give it a go and l look forward to hearing the stories about how it's worked for you.

By sharing this knowledge, I have helped people mend relationships, attract things and experiences simply by trusting in the dreaming process.

When I started using *The Secret*, I started with some of the simple suggestions outlined in the book and started with little things like attracting parking spots. I now love to use the law of attraction to attract parking spots. It may sound silly; however, I really do visualise and thank the Universe for my perfect spot before even getting it. I just know that when I'm rocking up somewhere, as I'm approaching my destination, I start saying in my mind thank you for my perfect park and visualise somebody pulling out right at the moment when I need it.

If used properly, it works nearly every time.

Even little things like attracting a cup of coffee into your life is a great way to start. A few years ago, I left home without my purse or money and as I was driving along to work all I could think about was coffee.

My mind was wandering off and dreaming about this coffee. I could smell it and taste it.

As I entered my workplace, the lady behind the desk handed me a cup of coffee and said that her colleague bought it for someone who didn't show up. My jaw dropped and I was overwhelmed with gratitude. For the next half an hour, I enjoyed my cup of coffee and gave thanks to the Universe for bringing it to me.

How to Use the Law of Attraction:

Manifesting Good Health

If there's an area in your body that you want to improve, the best place to start is to focus on all the areas in your body that are working well and that you are grateful for. Start by writing a list of all the things you are thankful for. Giving thanks for your working legs that get you around each day, or your eyes that allow you to see and experience life.

Remember many people would give anything to have what you have.

If there is any area in your body that you want to heal, start by saying, *"Thank you for my healing,"* and say it over and over, close your eyes and visualise your healing and how you would feel when you're healed.

Believe in miracles!

I continue to give thanks for my beating heart. We often forget about these very important organs within our body that keep us healthy and alive.

The keywords to attract good health are 'thank you'.

The Universe picks up on that energy and sees how grateful you are for your healthy body and in turn, will give you more things to be grateful for. If you're suffering from a chronic health condition, don't tell people about the bad health and dwell on it or complain about it.

Always focus on the positives and give thanks.

An example of this is even a common cold or feeling run down; I often have to remind myself of this as it's human nature to tell someone or whinge; however, we need to quickly bring our minds back to being positive and focusing on the good things.

In the book, *The Secret*, they use the analogy of the genie who always says, *"Your wish is my command."*

This is how the Universe works; it will give you what you've asked for and what you're focusing on the most.

Manifesting Healthy Relationships

To manifest and attract healthy relationships, we need to focus on strengths.

If it's a partner that you want to improve your relationship with, you should start by giving thanks for all the things you appreciate. The more you focus your positive energy on the things that you appreciate about your partner, the Universe will in turn, magically, start to give you more things to be grateful for.

It's human nature to thrive on encouragement and positivity.

Find it in your heart to focus on their strengths and say thank you for any little thing.

Close your eyes and visualise what you want to see. If you want to have more social time where you can enjoy that special time with your partner, then close your eyes and visualise it. Imagine laughing, going out for dinner or a drink (post COVID of course haha). Smile and give thanks for those things – the Universe will deliver the circumstances in order for you to experience those things.

They talk about the Universe not having a specific time frame so there's no way of knowing how long these things will take. It could take a few days, it could take a few months, or it could take a few years; my only suggestion is that you move forward with positivity in your heart and focus on all of the positive things in your life.

If you have a child with whom you have a strained relationship, perhaps they continue to be disrespectful, which completely drives you nuts. Much of this is out of your control as you can't control their actions; however, you can control your thoughts, energy and how you respond.

Just like you would with a spouse, by focusing on the strengths, this too is how you attract better relationships with your children. Focus on all the little things that you are thankful for. Let them know you see and acknowledge them. Smile at them and tell them you're proud of them. Even if it's for simple tasks, those two words – thank you – actually have a very powerful impact when it comes to using the law of attraction and attracting your best possible life.

Close your eyes and imagine your child or young person behaving the way you want them to. Imagine yourself smiling and being so grateful when you have attracted this perfect relationship into your life, give it some time and create the picture – just like a movie in your mind. Imagine the perfect situation and relationship and watch it unfold in real life.

I once had a supervisor who was horrible and very nasty at times. This particular person chose to find any little thing to pick on me about. She wouldn't respond when I greeted her in the morning and chose to deliberately leave me out of things. I let it go the first few times, thinking that she must have been having a bad day; however, I soon noticed that her behaviour was continuing and having a very negative impact on me.

I felt anxious, sad and confused and I wanted it to stop. It was affecting my joy in the workplace. I knew that I couldn't control the energy that she was putting out; however, I knew that I had the power to manifest the change that I wanted to see.

I started to visualise her smiling at me and being kind and praising me for my work. I didn't want to become friends with her; however, I just wanted her to leave me alone, so I could get on with my job. Within a couple of weeks, I noticed that her energy had shifted. She was no longer picking on me. All of a sudden, she magically just left me alone. She started to smile and greet me in the morning and compliment me on my work.

That's just a little yarn about how you can shift your own energy to manifest and improve relationships in your life.

Manifesting Money

Attracting money is a big one as we all need and want money to come into our lives, purely to meet our basic needs. The key to attracting money is to simply to think in abundance. I know that this is hard to comprehend; once you've read *The Secret* or watched the film, you will know what I mean.

If we have continuous bills that are coming into our lives that are making us stressed and anxious, the more we focus on these bills and increase our anxiety, the more bills we are going to receive.

I just visualise attracting money.

I expect that money will continue to flow into my life. I simply say in my mind over and over thank you for my money, thank you for the continuous abundance of resources, and magically, it keeps flowing in, allowing me to support my family and work towards my dreams and goals.

Visualise unexpected money coming into your account; close your eyes and give thanks for the money. The Universe always delivers in mysterious ways. It could be through winning money, finding money, someone gifting you something that you need or attracting a job that will allow an abundance of money to flow into your life. It sounds crazy, but I encourage you to give it ago.

Say out loud, *"Thank you, thank you, thank you for the abundance of money that continues to flow into my life!"*

Smile up real big and know that you are divinely protected and a magnet for all things positive.

We Are Only Limited by Our Imagination

I hope you're starting to get an idea of the way this works. It's all about manifesting, dreaming up and visualising what you want to achieve in life.

You can apply the same principles to many other areas in your life. Always remember that if somebody else can learn something or do something, then so can you.

We are only limited by our imagination and the belief in our ability to succeed.

Even though it scares us, we need to live life and have a go. I often have to remind myself of this, too.

Life is about living and continuously reflecting on where we are and where we want to be.

It's never too late to start something new. Ask for a sign and work towards finding your purpose.

I see myself as a lifelong learner who continuously tries to reflect and grow both personally and professionally. There are always lessons to be learnt from every experience, even those ones that shake and rattle us. Know that the Universe is always sending us challenges and obstacles to overcome. We are often guided or led on a particular path for a reason; even when things don't turn out the way we hope.

I know this is hard to comprehend at times. I believe there is always a lesson or a purpose for everything.

> "Whether you think you can or think you can't, either way, you are right."
> (Henry Ford)

Chapter Twelve

WHAT I KNOW FOR SURE

This final chapter is inspired by the incredible Oprah Winfrey, someone I have admired for many years and was lucky enough to see in person during her Australian tour a few years ago. Everything she says resonates with me so profoundly.

She is strong, courageous and inspirational, and throughout my journey, I have learnt so much from her inspiring words. Her book, *What I Know For Sure,* is one of my absolute favourites.

Oprah beautifully shares her insights into life and all the things she knows for sure, to inspire and touch the hearts of others. If anyone is reading this book and knows Oprah, please hook a sista up as I'd love to meet her.

In tribute to Oprah, here are the things I know for sure:

Old-Fashioned Blackfulla Curry Chicken Soup is Good for the Soul

There is nothing I love more than a good old-fashioned soup. My black brothers and sistas will know what I mean. It is a cure for any hangover, sickness and often a taste that will bring back so many childhood memories. I grew up on soup, and as an adult, it is still my favourite food. It reminds me of Mum. She loved my soups, and there was nothing more that I loved than making them for her.

You Only Live Once

You only live once (YOLO) is a term that gets thrown around a lot these days. It's a term that we should take seriously. This is particularly true for my mob, as sadly, our life expectancy is not as long as our non-Aboriginal brothers and sisters. My birth mum was 28, my sister, 30, Mum Denise, 59, and Nan was 65. That's not even retirement age these days. Reflecting on this has inspired me to make the most of every day I have here in this world. You should, too.

How Will You Leave Your Mark on the World?

How do you want to be remembered?

What is the legacy that you want to leave behind?

Do you want to be someone that made a difference in the lives of others?

Do you want to be remembered as someone who was resilient, despite the many challenges that life threw your way?

There are endless opportunities to do good in this world. I want to get to the end of my life knowing that I was brave and resilient and that I touched the hearts of others.

Get Outside and Just Breathe

There is something magical about the colours green and blue that bring peace and comfort. If you're feeling stressed or overwhelmed, don't stay inside and let it sit with you. Try to shake it off. Try getting out and going for a walk around the block or to the local park. Look out on the horizon and reflect on how truly blessed you are.

Feel the nice, cool breeze on your skin. Look up at the sky and take in the beauty of the colour blue. Look around and see the trees softly swaying in the wind. Look at how strong their roots are, buried deep within the ground. Despite the many storms and hot summers they've endured, they are still standing strong.

Think about others around the world who may not have access to this peace and safety. Breathe and take in the beauty. Take a deep breath in and hold it, focus on the area where you feel anxiety and then let it go. I often do this when I can't shake the stress.

What You Speak You Become

The law of attraction states that what you speak, feel and think, you'll become. So, complaining about and talking about your problems are only going to attract more problems. Choose to focus on things you are grateful for.

Gossiping Is Bad for Your Health

Whilst it's in our human nature to vent and criticise others who annoy us, What I Know For Sure, is that there are more important and positive things we can choose to focus our energy on. Wouldn't that make for a better yarn?

Start and End Your Day With the Words "Thank You"

Those two words are extremely powerful and have a magical way of shifting your focus to the positive things in your life. Think about all the little things that you're thankful for and express gratitude and appreciation for them. The Universe will bring you more things to be grateful for.

Being Around Children Brings You Joy

There is something magical about the innocence of children. Their smiles, the things they say and do and how they just cruise through life with joy and happiness without a care in the world. I love their energy which is why I light up and feel in my element in their company. If you need some uplifting, go and talk to a child. Even just thinking about a child can melt your heart.

There Is Something Magical About a Cup of Tea

Just like chicken soup, a cup of tea is good for the soul. It's cheap and readily available. A nice cup of tea brings back memories of my childhood. Nan was an avid tea drinker and we shared many yarns over a cuppa. She would drink countless cups every day with two tablespoons of sugar and powdered milk. A hit at breakfast was always tea and toast. There was something soothing about taking a piece of toast, smothering it in butter and dipping it into a hot cup of tea. It's even better when someone else makes it for you – but maybe go easy on the sugar and butter as we know that stuff isn't good for us.

It's Okay to Make Mistakes

Everyone makes mistakes, and it's okay to admit if you've made one. In fact, it's a credit to your character if you are brave enough to say you've made a mistake. Don't ever be afraid of admitting you are wrong. No one is perfect, and the word sorry is there for a reason. If you've made a mistake, admit it, apologise and move on.

Smiling at a Stranger Can Make Their Day

I am quite a social person and love to yarn. I'm also someone who is kind and friendly. I often smile and say hello to strangers in the street. I love seeing their faces light up through this simple act of kindness.

A few months ago, when I was feeling quite anxious, I decided to go out for a walk and breathe through the stress that had set in. I walked along the street with my head down, not paying attention to what was going on, then out of nowhere, I heard a voice. The voice of a kind man who politely said hello and smiled at me. It was enough to bring my attention back to my current situation. I looked up, smiled back and said hello. We then engaged in a conversation about the bottles he was collecting for the *Return and Earn* program. I enjoyed every moment yarning with this old man who changed my day with that simple gesture.

Compliments Make a Difference to Someone's Life

Nick Vujicic is an incredible inspirational speaker who I have grown to love over the years. He shared a video where he was talking about bullying to high school students. Nick was born with no arms and no legs and has found his resilience despite the difficult cards he was dealt. He is now an inspirational author, speaker, husband and father.

Nick shared a story about an experience from primary school, where kids would say nasty things about his appearance. He went through life feeling different, and the kids around him took every opportunity to let him know how different he was. Nick had tried to take his own life by drowning himself in the bath. He often questioned why God punished him in such way. Nick is now a man of God who knows his purpose.

Nick shared an example about a day at school when he had been bullied continuously throughout the day. He counted the number of times kids said mean things. With each comment, his confidence and self-worth slowly drained away. He said to himself that if he received one more negative comment then that was going to be the day he would go home and take his life. He was only 10 at the time.

As he was leaving the school grounds in his wheelchair, he heard a girl call out to him, *"Hey Nick!"*

He thought to himself, *"This is it. This is going to be the one."*

To his surprise, she said, *"I just want to let you know that you're looking good today."*

He was grinning from ear to ear, and all of a sudden, his fear and anxiety had melted away. That little girl made his day.

Be kind and compassionate as you never know what someone else is going through. It doesn't hurt to give a compliment and say something nice to someone – you just may make their day or save someone's life.

Focus on the Strengths

As a teacher, parent, spouse or leader, never be afraid to notice the effort those around us are putting in. Acknowledge them for their work and say thank you. As a giver of compliments and praise, it is a beautiful feeling for those on the receiving end, as it leaves them feeling valued and appreciated.

Don't Be Afraid to Try Something New

I have always been someone to live my life in the safe lane. Not wanting to take risks or try something new, I soon realised that I was missing out on so many things that life had to offer. My brother-in-law, Cass, once told me what to do when I get scared. It was simple and laughable. He told me to get unscared.

He was right.

I needed to stop living my life being scared. I found the courage to try new things, such as travelling to countries I always labelled dangerous. Once I got unscared, I realised there was so much joy to be had experiencing the simple things in life.

I recently went hot air ballooning with friends. The old me was scared; however, the unscared me decided to give it a go. Although I spent the entire 45 minutes praying and visualising touching down safely, I did enjoy the views and was so proud of myself for agreeing to the opportunity.

I'm not saying go and be a risk-taker and engage in things that may cause you harm; I'm saying to go through life with an open mind, knowing that many experiences just may bring us happiness – that thing we're all chasing.

Now Is Your Time to Shine

Sometimes getting out of our comfort zone is difficult but when we do, the joy that it brings is at times indescribable.

If you get the chance to dance and enjoy life – do it! Dance like nobody's watching.

I encourage you to write a list of the things that you know for sure.

I'd love for you to share yours in our *Dream Big and Imagine the What If* Facebook group so we can continue to inspire each other and keep the fire burning in our bellies. Remember that we are magnificent human beings who are capable of achieving anything that our heart desires.

Now is your time to shine.

Never has there been a better time than now. Don't be shame. Turn up and work towards living the life of your dreams.

Break the cycle and be the change you want to see.

Join me in saying this affirmation, *"I am divinely protected and continuously being guided. The Universe will never send me obstacles that I can't handle. I express gratitude for every blessing in my life. I surrender to all the Universe has planned for me. I call on my spirit guides to support me in this journey of life. I forgive myself for I am not perfect, and I forgive others who have caused sadness in my life. I open my heart and mind and ask the Universe to help me live out my purpose. Send me the people, circumstances and events to show me the way. I am strong and resilient, and I am ready."*

Keep an eye out for the signs. Simple things like this book landing in your hands or the fact that you've made it all the way to the end is a credit to you. It makes me smile knowing that I have found the courage to share my journey with you.

Find your purpose and move forward with love, hope and positivity, knowing you are continuously being guided.

Take action and embark on your journey of dreaming up the life of your dreams.

I would love to hear from you. Please reach out and let me know your thoughts on my book following this experience that you have gifted yourself.

It would bring me so much joy if you shared what resonated with you most.

I love you, I believe in you and I'm grateful for you.

With sincere gratitude and appreciation for allowing me to share my story with you.

Your dreams are only a thought away –
imagine the 'what if'.

Stay proud and stay deadly.

Kylie x

Kylie is now a passionate educator, speaker and author.

Kylie speaking at the Aboriginal Student Achievement Awards

Kylie getting ready to appear as a panellist on ABC's *The Drum*

What I Know For Sure

Kylie speaking at a school NAIDOC event where she was presented with a beautiful personalised gift that said 'dream'

DREAM BIG & Imagine the What If

Allira's Year 12 school photo – 2021
One of Kylie's prodest moments as a mother
was watching her children attain their HSC

Tyrell's Year 12 photo – 2018

ABOUT THE AUTHOR

Kylie Captain is a proud Aboriginal woman from Sydney, Australia. Her people are from Gamilaroi Country, a small country town called Walgett in North West New South Wales. Kylie has a strong connection to the land of the Gadigal people where she was born and raised in the inner-city suburbs of Redfern and Waterloo.

Kylie is a primary school teacher and an educational leader. She has a deep understanding of pedagogical knowledge to engage Aboriginal students and has extensive experience presenting highly engaging professional learning for schools both locally and at educational conferences across New South Wales.

As a result of Kylie's extensive experience, she has emerged as a confident and engaging public speaker.

Kylie is the Vice President of the Aboriginal Studies Association and over the past 20 years, has had an impressive career working in finance, community services and education.

Sadly, Kylie has experienced more unimaginable loss and challenging moments than anyone should ever have to encounter. She attributes her success to the law of attraction and the power of education. Kylie's dream is to pay it forward by sharing her love of education in hope that every student will know that they can achieve anything they set their mind to. She wants them to know how deadly they are and that with a strong mindset, they can achieve anything their heart desires.

Kylie's greatest source of strength is her Aboriginality. She attributes her success to her connection to culture and spirituality which has led her to live a rich and fulfilling life on her terms.

Once thinking she was not good enough or smart enough to succeed in life, Kylie is now an inspirational leader and speaker who has created a life beyond what she could have ever imagined.

Kylie's resilience and determination has inspired many. Her passion and commitment is highlighted in all she does. She dedicates her life to improving outcomes for Aboriginal students and inspiring anyone to recognise their potential, believe in themselves and chase their dreams.

ABOUT THE ARTIST (BOOK COVER)

Campbelltown-based Aboriginal artist Michael Fardon holds a Bachelor of Visual Arts from the University of Western Sydney. Michael is a Dharawal man and self-taught artist who lives and works on Country using a range of styles and mediums, including painting and digital formats. Michael works closely with communities and schools to create collaborative mural art with Aboriginal students.

WANT MORE?

- Purchase your Dream Big Journal from *kyliecaptain.com.au* to start your journey of dreaming big and imagining the 'what if'

- Head to *kyliecaptain.com.au* to download your free goal setting tool

- Like Kylie's social media pages by searching for *'Kylie Captain'*

- Join Kylie's Facebook group by searching for *'Dream Big and Imagine the What If'*

- Keep an eye out for Kylie's Dream Big Masterclass if you'd like to learn more

ACKNOWLEDGEMENTS

I acknowledge and thank my beautiful angels and ancestors who continue to guide and comfort me in spirit, thank you for your ongoing love and protection.

I hope I've made you proud.

There are so many people to thank for their love and support over the years.

To my children, who are my everything. Thank you for choosing me to be your mum. My life changed for the better when you came into my life.

Tyrell, you came into my life at a time when I needed you most. You saved me from a life of self-destruction and have been my strength and inspiration in all I do. We have grown and taken on many of life's challenges together. Continue to dream big and always remember that you are capable of anything you set your mind to. Thank you for being the most incredible son. I love you.

Allira, my beautiful daughter, best friend and mini-me. You are always in my heart, mind and spirit in everything I do. When I look at you, I see myself. Smart, kind and compassionate. Thank you for being the best daughter any mother could ask for. Continue to dance and shine bright, my darling. Carry the strength of our ancestors with you in all you do. I love you always and forever, my princess.

To my incredible husband, Jamie. I love you more than you know. Your unconditional love and support have allowed me to follow my dreams to be where I am today. Without you, none of this would be possible. Thank you for your encouragement and for always believing in me. I know that together we can do anything and I thank God every day for sending you to me.

A special thanks to my beautiful friend Zia and amazing cousins Annelise and Bronwyn who have supported me through my writing journey. Those times when the fear set in, you reminded me that my story was worth sharing and encouraged me to keep going. Without you, I don't think I would have made it this far.

To all my beautiful nieces and nephews, those through blood and those I've claimed along the way. There are too many to mention. Thank you for the joy you bring to my life. It's your beautiful faces I see when I show up and do what I do every day. Always remember to dream big and know you are

Acknowledgements

capable of achieving anything you set your mind to. Aunty Ky loves you all so much.

To all of my family and friends, the special people in my life who have supported my journey. I'll never have the right words to truly express my gratitude and appreciation to you all.

To my incredible work family, both past and present. I love and appreciate you all. To my St George, Lakemba, Sackville St, Arncliffe and Glenfield mob, thank you for all the years of friendship and support. I love and appreciate you all.

A special thank you to Melinda Smith at Heavens Above for the years of support, healing and guidance. I appreciate all the beautiful messages and words of encouragement. Without the continuous reminders and nudges, none of this would be possible.

Thank you to my friends George and Robyn at HOW Strategy Group for the years of support with finance approvals. You guys were there to bring many of my dreams to life.

I could write a book just thanking all the special people in my life. You know who you are. Thank you for your unconditional love and support.

Last but not least, to Nat, Stu and the team at Ultimate 48 Hour Author. Thank you for giving me the push I needed to bring this dream to life. I am forever grateful.

I am beyond blessed for all the love and support in my life. Thank you, thank you, thank you.

GLOSSARY

Blackfullas – Aboriginal or Torres Strait Islander people of Australia

Deadly – Awesome, fantastic, great

Cones – To smoke marijuana

Flash – Fancy, stunning, impressive

Gammon – Fake, pretend, to joke or muck around, not good

Lore – Customs, stories, traditions, rules of living

Mob – Family, kin

Score – To purchase drugs

Shame – Embarrassed, shy, not confident

Sista – Friend, colleague, cousin or any female, sometimes Aboriginal and non-Aboriginal

Whanau – Maori word for family

Whitefullas – White Australians

Womba – Crazy, mad

Yarndi – Marijuana

Yarns – Oral stories, conversations

KYLIE'S DEADLY CHICKEN SOUP

Ingredients

- Whole chicken
- Keen's Curry Powder (this is the key ingredient – no other curry powder will do. Blackfullas love Keen's Curry)
- Massel Chicken Stock powder
- Salt
- Cornflour
- Potato
- Pumpkin
- Onion
- Carrot
- Zucchini
- Capsicum
- Spinach
- Cabbage
- Optional: Any veggies you like

Chicken Soup

Place whole chicken in a pot, cover with water and sprinkle with salt. Bring to the boil and simmer for an hour. Dice veggies and place in a separate pot. Cover with water. Add 1 tbsp of chicken stock and 1 tbsp of curry powder. Sprinkle with salt and bring to the boil. Simmer for about 45 minutes until potatoes are cooked. Cook a pot of rice if you wish.

When chicken is cooked, keep 2–3 cups of broth to add to the veggie pot for flavour. Run cold water over the chicken to cool. Pull chicken into pieces. Dispose of skin as it makes for an oily soup. Combine cooked vegetables and pulled chicken into one pot.

Depending on how much spice you like, add extra curry accordingly. I use about 2–3 tablespoons in addition to the one already added to the veggies. Add 1–2 more tablespoons of chicken stock to the pot. Stir and taste – add extra curry or stock if needed.

To thicken, add 2 tbsp of cornflour to water. Stir and make sure any bumps have been smoothed out. Pour into soup to thicken. If you don't have cornflour, plain flour is okay. Stir and taste.

Doughboys

Pour 3 to 4 cups of self-raising flour into bowl. Sprinkle with salt. Use half milk/half water to combine. Slowly add to flour while combining. Add extra milk or flour until you have a dough-like consistency. Roll into balls and add to simmering soup.

Cook doughboys for five minutes. They should be fluffy and bread like.

To Serve

Add rice, soup and doughboys to bowl. Sprinkle with salt and pepper to taste and enjoy.

FURTHER TESTIMONIALS

'"I am good enough and I am smart enough. I'm healthy and full of love and life. I forgive myself for not being perfect, as no one is. I trust the journey of life and know that everything that I have experienced has led me to where I am today.' (Kylie Captain)

If you have ever felt not good enough, struggled with your self-image and self-doubt, failure, taken the wrong path, or wrestled with grief, this story will speak volumes to you and lift you, inspiring you to redefine yourself. It will help you reset and redirect you to a positive path. It is a courageous story that inspires and demonstrates how to harness your own resilience in order to achieve great things.

Kylie Captain's personal story is deeply honest, full of heart and demonstrates her grit to not only live but thrive. Kylie leads us through her raw and deeply personal story guiding us all in understanding how we too can dream big, imagine the 'what ifs' and achieve our life goals. She provides a road map for improving our outlook on life, demonstrating how to rise above challenges and setbacks, deal with grief and create the life we all deserve. Kylie bares her soul sharing personal experiences to show us how it's never too late to develop a goal and to visualise the life that we have always dreamt. Her bravery in overcoming multiple setbacks, her ability to love and trust despite losing almost every loved one at an early age is heartbreaking but this does not stop her; it instead lights a fire in her belly to rise above it, all while inspiring others to do so too. Empowered to live her life to the fullest, she honours her past, faces her fears head on and not only chases her dream but achieves them.

It is a beautiful reminder that our past does not define us but is rather a part of our journey. Kylie demonstrates how to change the inner voice to one of self-belief. As an educator she also advocates for not only her people but for everyone. Kylie writes from the heart, with courage, kindness and a drive to have a positive impact on all she comes in contact with in her endeavour to leave the world a better place. She encourages the reader to draw upon their resilience to unlock and unleash their potential. 'Dream Big and Imagine the What If' is a must read, a true narrative that gives great insights into transforming yourself to lead the life you have always imagined. She provides practical advice by stimulating self-reflection, thought and will leave you changed for the better. A heart-wrenching story of hope and resilience empowering others to greatness.

I am forever grateful that our paths crossed as Kylie inspires and encourages me too to advocate for our children, to give gratitude for all that is great and most of all to strive to be the best version of myself. I hope that is your experience too as you interact with this passionate and resilient author. A story that goes beyond hope!"

Narelle Nies
Educational Leader

Further Testimonials

"'Dream Big and Imagine the What If' took me on an emotional and eye-opening journey, and it has been a book I just couldn't put down! Each chapter resonated with my own experiences of grief, my work as a teacher, my interest in Aboriginal culture, and my continual journey of self-discovery and improvement.

I've read Kylie's book multiple times and each time I've gained new insights into the powerful topics she explores. I admire and am inspired by Kylie's raw, authentic and genuine writing style in which she opens up about the many challenges she has faced and overcome.

I was inspired to work on my passions and goals through self-belief, hard work, positivity and, most importantly, kindness. Kylie gave me the understanding of why these are important things to aim for as well as providing clear steps to continually improve in these areas.

After reading *Dream Big and Imagine the What If*, in the words of Kylie, 'I will continue to do my part in making a difference for the change I wish to see.'"

Annelise Dixon
Teacher

"This is a wonderful and critically important read.

Kylie is a proud Gamillaroi woman whose vulnerability and honesty about her life's journey overcoming addiction and navigating unimaginable loss is inspiring and uplifting.

As for so many First Nations People, her family's health and wellbeing have been devastated by the legacy of attempted genocide and ongoing racism. Kylie does not dwell on these injustices. Instead she writes beautifully about love, family, connection, kinship and community and how this kept her strong and helped her to persevere through her darkest moments to achieve huge success in her life.

Kylie has chosen to share parts of her story in the hope that her words and the love behind them can help others. It is a privilege to read and easy to understand why Kylie is a role model to so many.

Reading this book has me reflecting on the What If. What if non-Aboriginal people could listen and learn from stories like these and take meaningful action to move towards justice, truth, equality and healing for First Nations People. *Dream Big and Imagine the What If* is essential reading for all Australians.

Read it and then buy several more copies for your family and friends. This is a voice that matters."

Zia Tayebjee
Social Worker

Further Testimonials

"Some people make an unforgettable first impression in a matter of minutes and you find they even exceed their reputation when you meet with them. Kylie is one of those people. Her ability to put people at ease, share her kindness and completely envelop you with her optimism, makes every encounter with her memorable.

Kylie has transcended disadvantage, profound grief and setbacks, making her well placed to guide anyone to see what is beautiful in life. This is where her thoughts and energy go, and success follows.

To be connected to culture, our Elders and pride in the achievements of Aboriginal people past, present and future gives Kylie strength and deep purpose.

As a gifted educator no matter who is in the room, Kylie is highly dedicated to addressing inequity and the closing of achievement gaps. However, there is another gap to close in Australia and it is the truth and knowledge gap of our Aboriginal people.

Kylie has an incredible ability to connect, educate and raise awareness so that other educators and leaders are well placed to teach with authenticity and confidence.

This book will inspire anyone who thinks rock bottom is down and out, to think differently. It will lead the reader to learn that rock bottom is a place to journey from with the right climbing tools: hope, compassion, purpose, pride and a dedicated love of children."

Kylie Lyneham
Aboriginal Educational Leader

"This book provides an incredible and indispensable insight into the subjects of grief, culture, kindness, education, community, endurance and mother's love. Kylie's journey of life lived to the fullest in 40 years. With breathtaking honesty and humility Kylie dives deep into her personal story of truth.

There is so much for everyone to learn and understand from the student to the teacher in life. Kylie has it fully covered from the first page to the end.

Direct experience in life is our greatest teacher to assist in these now times of living. Kylie's words of wisdom and love will capture your heart many times over throughout this book."

Melinda Smith
Counsellor and Life Coach, Heavens Above
Helensburgh

NOTES

www.ingramcontent.com/pod-product-compliance
Lightning Source LLC
Chambersburg PA
CBHW021143080526
44588CB00008B/191